The J. Paul Getty Museum

HANDBOOK *of the*
Collections

The J. Paul Getty Museum

HANDBOOK *of the*
Collections

LOS ANGELES

© 2001 J. Paul Getty Trust

Getty Publications
1200 Getty Center Drive
Suite 500
Los Angeles, California
90049-1682
www.getty.edu

Sixth Edition
Second printing

Library of Congress
Cataloging-in-Publication
Data

J. Paul Getty Museum.
The J. Paul Getty Museum
handbook of the collections.
p. cm.
Rev. ed. of: The J. Paul
Getty Museum handbook
of the collections, 1997.
ISBN 0-89236-613-3
ISBN 978-0-89236-613-2
(cloth) —
ISBN 0-89236-614-1
ISBN 978-0-89236-614-9
(pbk.)
1. Art — California —
Los Angeles — Catalogs.
2. J. Paul Getty Museum —
Catalogs. I. Title:
Handbook of the collec-
tions. II. Title.
N582.M25 A627 2001
708.194'93 — dc21
00-062842

Printed and bound in
Singapore

Publisher
Christopher Hudson

Managing Editor
Mark Greenberg

Editor
Mollie Holtman

Production Coordinator
Elizabeth Zozom

Designer
Jeffrey Cohen

Photographers
Charles Passela
Jack Ross
Lou Meluso
Ellen Rosenbery
Bruce White

Typesetter
G&S Typesetters, Inc.
Austin, Texas

Color Separator
Professional Graphics Inc.
Rockford, Illinois

Printer
CS Graphics, Inc.
Singapore

On the cover:
Paul Cézanne (French, 1839–
1906), *Young Italian Woman
at a Table*, circa 1895–1900
(detail). Oil on canvas,
91.7 × 73.3 cm (36⅛ × 28⅞
in.). 99.PA.40 (see p. 141).

On the back cover:
View of the Museum court-
yard at the Getty Center.
Photo: Scott Frances/Esto

On the title page:
Nicolas Poussin (French,
1594–1665), *Landscape with
a Calm*, 1650–51 (detail).
Oil on canvas, 97 × 131.5 cm
(39 × 52¼ in.). 97.PA.60
(see pp. 126–27).

Page VI:
Children take in *Christ's
Entry into Brussels in 1889*
by James Ensor (see pp.
148–49). Photo: Gary Moss

The Collections

Introduction

The Getty Museum has undergone a remarkable transformation since the most recent *Handbook of the Collections* appeared in 1997. A new museum at the Getty Center opened in December of that year to much acclaim and even more popularity—there were more than 1.7 million visitors in 1998, more than four times the previous annual attendance in Malibu. The buildings, designed by Richard Meier, provide new opportunities for both visitors and staff. With much more gallery space for the permanent collection, much more of the collection is on view. There is space for loan exhibitions, and already a varied and popular series of shows has been held. The quality of the galleries is greatly improved. Paintings have abundant daylight, the decorative arts have a splendid suite of rooms evoking the scale and interior design of the eighteenth century, and other works ranging from Renaissance bronze sculpture to twentieth-century photographs occupy rooms of appropriate scale and finish. A variety of education spaces and services have been placed throughout the new Museum to help visitors better understand and enjoy the collection. The building itself offers a constantly changing and refreshing experience for our visitors, allowing them to absorb the collection, as well as enjoy the architecture, the landscape, the views from the Getty Center, and (on most days) the weather.

The permanent collection is the core of everything the Museum does. We are fortunate in being able to add to it more and more important works, and have done so frequently since the last edition of the *Handbook*. "If a museum is alive and thriving, it is bound to keep changing and improving," wrote a former director, Stephen Garrett, in a guidebook of 1982. "This is good for our visitors and good for our staff. But it means that guidebooks go quickly out of date." That one did, and so have its successors, the 1986, 1988, 1991, and 1997 editions of the *Handbook of the Collections*. The rapid growth of the collection made possible by J. Paul Getty's huge bequest in 1976 could not have been imagined when the Getty Museum opened in 1954, or even when the Villa building opened in 1974. Since the early 1980s hundreds of important new works of art have been acquired in the areas of the Museum's three traditional interests, antiquities, French furniture and decorative arts, and European paintings, and thousands more have been acquired to form four new collections.

Classical antiquities, the largest of the Museum's original collections, was strengthened by the purchase of important groups of Greek vases,

Cycladic figures and vessels, Hellenistic metalwork, and sculpture from Magna Graecia. In 1996 one of the finest private collections of Greek and Roman works in existence, that of Lawrence and Barbara Fleischman, was acquired through donation and purchase.

J. Paul Getty had a particular passion for the exquisitely made furniture and decorative objects of eighteenth-century France. In recent years many more have been added in various periods, especially the Neoclassical. The entire collection now occupies an extensive suite of galleries and paneled rooms, a kind of museum-within-a-museum at the Getty Center.

The Getty's European paintings now include dozens of examples of very great importance, among them a group of Italian works of the Renaissance and many fine seventeenth-century Dutch paintings. There is a small but brilliant group of Impressionist and Post-Impressionist pictures. About 170 paintings have been added to the collection since 1983.

Entire collections have been formed in the past twenty years and four new curatorial departments created. The Museum has bought drawings since 1981; there are over 550 examples of remarkably high quality distributed across the history of European art. The collection ranks among the finest for its size in the world.

In 1983 the Museum entered the field of illuminated manuscripts with the purchase of the Ludwig Collection, 144 items that formed the most important group of medieval and Renaissance manuscripts in private hands; since then, over sixty-five acquisitions have made the Getty's collection far more diverse and important.

In 1984 the Museum seized another exceptional opportunity and bought a number of the best private holdings of photographs anywhere. Together with thousands of acquisitions made since then, they now form one of the world's finest collections of photographs. All the drawings, manuscripts, and photographs are available for study by students and scholars, and a selection of each is on view in changing exhibitions.

The Museum also has been actively buying European sculpture. Statues in bronze and marble of the sixteenth through the nineteenth century can now be seen in a series of ground-floor galleries in the new Museum together with maiolica, glass, goldsmiths' work, *pietre dure*, and Italian furniture.

One of our aims is to satisfy every visitor's curiosity, making a trip to the Getty Museum as much a memorable adventure for the mind as a delight for the senses. We offer information about the collection through many different means: introductory talks, lectures, publications, labels, didactic shows, audioguides, and interactive computer programs. And we offer to families and schools an ambitious program of services. With our visibility in Los Angeles and our much-expanded capacity, we try to ensure that those services are used to the fullest.

It is a rare American museum that is not under construction or renovation, and the Getty, despite having completed the Getty Center, is no exception. Extensive changes are underway at the site of the Getty Museum in Malibu (actually Pacific Palisades, in the city of Los Angeles), the reconstructed Roman villa that was operated as the J. Paul Getty Museum from 1974 to 1997. In the near future the Getty Villa will again become the permanent home for the J. Paul Getty Museum's collection of Greek, Roman, and Etruscan antiquities. Redesigned galleries will display more of the collection than was possible in the past, and other galleries will allow for loan exhibitions. A new auditorium, bookstore, and many new educational services will enrich the experience of visitors of all ages.

The Villa and its surrounding buildings and landscape are being renovated to designs by Machado and Silvetti Associates, Inc., in collaboration with Langdon Wilson, architects of the original Villa, with a more challenging mission in mind: to promote a broader understanding of, and critical appreciation for, the art of the Classical world, particularly in relation to other ancient cultures. This work will be pursued not only by the Museum staff but also by the Getty Research and Conservation Institutes, which will operate programs at the Villa. A library, seminar rooms, and offices for scholars will support innovative research programs that will lead to publications and exhibitions. Conservation laboratories will not only serve the needs of the Museum's Antiquities Conservation Department but will strengthen a new M.A. program for conservation of archaeological and ethnographic materials cosponsored by the Institute of Archaeology at the University of California, Los Angeles. There will also be new facilities for a varied menu of public programs including lectures, concerts, and theatrical performances. When it reopens, the Villa will be the only place in America dedicated solely to the exhibition, interpretation, and preservation of the world's archaeological heritage.

John Walsh, director since 1983 and ultimately responsible for much of what is contained in this volume, retired in October 2000. As it enters a new phase, the Museum and its collections will continue to bring pleasure and enlightenment to the public. May this book give readers who have not yet seen the original works of art an inducement for visiting the Getty Museum. For those who have, may it recall the experience and enrich the recollection.

Deborah Gribbon
Director

J. Paul Getty and His Legacy

J. Paul Getty combined the lives of oil-field wildcatter, shrewd and spectacularly successful businessman, writer, and member of the international art world. His attitude toward art and collecting was complex. Although he maintained that "fine art is the finest investment," he also felt that "few human activities provide an individual with a greater sense of personal gratification than the assembling of a collection of art objects that appeal to him and that he feels have a true and lasting beauty." When he died on June 6, 1976, at the age of eighty-three, Paul Getty had collected art for more than forty-five years. Collecting was a part of his life that he relished and about which he felt deeply.

J. Paul Getty (fig. 1) was born in 1892 in Minneapolis. His father, George F. Getty, was a successful attorney and already wealthy when he entered the oil business in Oklahoma in 1903. He planned to have Paul, his only child, enter the family business, and so Paul worked summers in the Oklahoma oil fields from the age of sixteen.

After a semester at the University of Southern California and time at the University of California, Berkeley, Getty began to read political science and economics at Oxford University in November 1912. He received his diploma in June 1913 and set off on a *Wanderjahr*. He made the rounds of museums and galleries from Sweden and Russia to Greece and Egypt but later could recall being impressed by only one painting—the *Venus* by Titian in the Uffizi.

After spending the tense early days of World War I in London with his parents, Getty began a trial year of joint ventures in the Oklahoma oil fields with his father. In 1916 he brought in his first producing oil well, becoming a millionaire at age twenty-three, and he returned to Los Angeles in July 1916 for an extended vacation. When the United States entered the war, he applied to the Army Air Service but was not called. He gradually adopted a pattern of living about seven months of the year in Europe and five months in the United States, where he helped make George F. Getty Incorporated, the family oil firm, increasingly profitable. When his

FIGURE 1

J. Paul Getty, 1960s. Photo: JPGM Archives

FIGURE 2

ROLLTOP DESK

French, circa 1788
Made by Bernard Molitor
(1758–1833)
Fir and oak veneered with
mahogany and ebony; gilt-
bronze mounts; marble top
137 × 181 × 87 cm
(4 ft. 6 in. × 5 ft. 11½ in. ×
2 ft. 10¼ in.)
Los Angeles, J. Paul Getty
Museum 67.DA.9

father died in May 1930, Getty became president. Perhaps as a relief from
his business responsibilities, he found his interest in art developing. He read
voraciously on the subject and visited museums whenever he could.

The United States and Europe were enjoying a period of tremendous
prosperity, and great numbers of wealthy collectors—including William
Randolph Hearst, the Mellons, and the Rothschilds—bid against each other
enthusiastically for anything great that came on the market. Following the
panic of 1929 and the Depression, Getty found that the time was right to
begin collecting works of art. In March 1931 he purchased his first art object
of value—a landscape by the seventeenth-century Dutch painter Jan van
Goyen—at auction in Berlin for about $1,100. Two years later he bought
ten paintings by the Spanish Impressionist Joaquin Sorolla y Bastida at a
New York auction.

Getty often said that he was inspired to collect decorative arts after
leasing a penthouse in 1936 from a Mrs. Frederick Guest on Sutton Place

FIGURE 3

THE ARDABIL
CARPET

Persian, Safavid Dynasty,
1540
Made by Maqsud Kashani
Wool
729 × 409 cm
(23 ft. 11 in. × 13 ft. 5 in.)
Los Angeles County
Museum of Art 53.50.2,
Gift of J. Paul Getty

South in New York. The apartment was furnished with French and English eighteenth-century pieces, and Getty responded enthusiastically to living with them. He acquired in one stroke the beginnings of a significant collection of French eighteenth-century furniture at the Mortimer Schiff sale in London in June 1938. Fear of impending war kept bidding far below estimates. Among the purchases were a magnificent Savonnerie carpet, the famous Rolltop Desk by Bernard Molitor (fig. 2), two round tables with Sèvres porcelain plaques by Martin Carlin, and a settee with four chairs by Jean-Jacques-Baptiste Tilliard *fils*. The Ardabil Carpet (fig. 3), a large sixteenth-century Persian carpet made to adorn the most holy of all the Persian religious shrines, the Safi-ud-din, was acquired from the personal collection of Lord Duveen.

FIGURE 4

REMBRANDT
HARMENSZ.
VAN RIJN

Dutch, 1606–1669
Portrait of Marten Looten,
1632
Oil on panel
92.7 × 76.2 cm (36½ × 30 in.)
Los Angeles County
Museum of Art 53.50.3,
Gift of J. Paul Getty

In succeeding months Getty bought a large number of paintings, the
start of the Museum's collection. He bid anonymously on Rembrandt's
Portrait of Marten Looten (fig. 4) at the sale of the Anton W. W. Mensing
in the Netherlands, then lent the portrait anonymously for exhibit in the
Fine Arts Pavilion of the 1939 New York World's Fair. This enabled him
"to share his joy in owning the masterpiece with millions of people."

World War II temporarily curtailed Getty's collecting. He threw his
energies into expanding and running the Spartan Aircraft Corporation
in Tulsa, manufacturing aircraft and training pilots. By 1947 he was back in
Europe, living in hotel rooms and negotiating deals with the burgeoning
European oil market and for the development of oil fields in North Africa
and Arabia. A fully integrated worldwide oil network—producing, trans-
porting, refining, and marketing—soon made Getty's company a strong
competitor to the giants of the oil world.

Getty's avocation continued to be art. He visited museums, archaeological sites, and art dealers, recording in his diary works of art that
impressed him (and often their prices). In the early 1950s he resumed
buying art and began donating works from his collection to various museums, including the Santa Barbara Museum of Art, Oberlin College, and
the San Diego Museum of Art. In 1953 he gave the Los Angeles County
Museum of Art two of his most prized possessions, the Rembrandt *Portrait*

of Marten Looten and the Ardabil Carpet. Later in 1953, colleagues, notably Norris Bramlett, persuaded him to establish a museum in his own name. The ranch Getty had purchased in Los Angeles in 1945 seemed an ideal location. The trust indenture he executed in late 1953, the only document in which he specified how his money was to be used, authorized the creation of a "museum, gallery of art and library" and stated the purpose of the trust simply as "the diffusion of artistic and general knowledge."

In the early fifties Getty made his first important purchases of antiquities: the life-size marble Lansdowne Herakles (see p. 26), three sculptures from the Earl of Elgin's collection at Broomhall including the Elgin Kore (fig. 5), and the fifth-century-B.C. Cottenham Relief. Greek and Roman sculpture was to be a continuing passion for Getty; the Herakles remained a personal favorite until the end of his life.

FIGURE 5

S T A T U E   O F   A
F E M A L E   F I G U R E

(The Elgin Kore)
Greek, circa 475 B.C.
Gray marble
71 × 28 × 19 cm
(28 × 11 × 7½ in.)
Los Angeles, J. Paul Getty
Museum 70.AA.114

The J. Paul Getty Museum was opened to the public in May 1954 (fig. 6). Although Getty continued to buy works of art for his private residences, the best pieces began to appear in the Museum, which also acquired a small staff. The distinguished art historian Wilhelm R. Valentiner was made director in 1954 and remained for two years. George F. Getty II, Getty's eldest son, became director shortly after Dr. Valentiner and remained until his death in 1973. Getty himself then served as director until he died.

In the mid-fifties Getty tried to build all three of his collections—paintings, decorative arts, and antiquities—with some consistency. He met the famous connoisseur Bernard Berenson and passed much time talking with him and studying art in the library at Villa I Tatti in Settignano, not far from Florence. Under Berenson's influence, Getty began to take an interest in Italian Renaissance painting and to acquire Italian pictures to add to his Dutch and English paintings. His thoughts on art and the art market at this time are expressed in *Collector's Choice*, a book he wrote with Ethel LeVane in 1955. His approach to collecting was a simple one: "I buy the things I like—and I like the things I buy—the true collector's guiding philosophy."

Getty enjoyed research and tried to be certain his acquisitions were thoroughly studied, often employing scholars to determine the provenances and former prices of works of art he was considering and give opinions about them. Competent in six languages—English, French, Spanish, German, Italian, and Latin—Getty had an approach to research that was both wide-ranging and individual. He frequently lamented that he lacked sufficient leisure to follow up all the clues.

In some ways Getty saw himself in the tradition of other ambitious and eclectic collectors, from the Roman emperor Hadrian to his own older contemporary William Randolph Hearst. In his diary Getty compared the architecture and investments represented by Hadrian's Villa and Hearst Castle at San Simeon with his own holdings in art and real estate. He was gratified to own works of art that great connoisseurs of the past had owned and cherished.

In October 1957 an article in *Fortune* magazine listed Getty, until then a virtually unknown businessman, as the richest American. From then on the American public began to use the Getty name as a synonym for wealth. At times Getty was uncomfortable with the attention paid to his personal fortune and tried to deflect it into discussions of the number of jobs his corporations created through reinvestment of profits. In 1957 a gallery was added to the small museum in Malibu, and all the recently purchased antiquities and decorative arts purchases were installed (fig. 7).

FIGURE 6
The Ranch House, Malibu, California, circa 1950s. Photo: JPGM Archives

FIGURE 7
Antiquities gallery in the Ranch House, circa 1965. Photo: JPGM Archives

FIGURE 8
Sutton Place, Surrey, England. Photo: JPGM Archives

Much of Getty's attention between 1958 and 1968 was centered on
Sutton Place, a manor house twenty-five miles southwest of London
built in 1521–26 by one of Henry VIII's courtiers. The house was acquired
in 1959 by a subsidiary of the Getty Oil Company to serve as the parent
company's new international headquarters and as Getty's own residence
(fig. 8). He continued to acquire art. One major purchase, made in 1962, was
the Rembrandt *Saint Bartholomew* (see pp. 120–121), in 1962.

By 1967 he had resumed buying at auctions. His interest in the Getty
Museum also revived, and in the coming years he earmarked large sums
for the purchase of works of art, notably the portrait of Agostino Pallavicini
by Anthony van Dyck (see p. 114).

During 1968 Getty decided to expand his Museum. Gradually he
developed the idea of a major art museum that he could leave as a gift to
the people of Los Angeles. "There were other, and for me, overriding
considerations," he wrote. "It was my intent that the collections should be
completely open to the public, free of all charges be they for admission or
even for parking automobiles. Nothing of this sort could be insured
if the museum were under the control of a city, state, or even the Federal
government."

One evening at Sutton Place Getty announced to a group of guests
that he wished to build a separate large building on the ranch property and
that it was to be an accurate re-creation of the Villa dei Papiri in Hercula-

neum. The villa had been one of the largest ever built in the ancient Roman Empire and had possibly been owned by Lucius Calpurnius Piso, father-in-law of Julius Caesar. The villa had stood outside Herculaneum on the Bay of Naples and had been buried along with that city and Pompeii when Mount Vesuvius erupted in A.D. 79. Getty had eagerly pored over the scanty information about the villa's architecture. It would satisfy his desire for a museum building that would itself be a work of art. To this end he eventually invested more than $17 million in a new building and endowed the Museum to meet operating expenses.

Ground was broken in December 1970, and three intense years of work (fig. 9) produced the results that have delighted more than four hundred thousand visitors a year ever since (fig. 10). During construction Getty and the trustees realized that the new building would provide an enormous increase in gallery space. From 1970 to 1974, a large number of works of art were purchased and the professional staff was enlarged. The British architect Stephen Garrett joined the staff to oversee the project; he became assistant director, and then, after Getty's death, director until 1983.

The new J. Paul Getty Museum building opened its doors to the public in January 1974. Greek and Roman art set the tone because of the architecture and gardens, and the entire main floor was devoted to antiquities. Although this part of the collection was of great importance, relative to other museums the French furniture was the finest of the three Getty collections, with paintings remaining the least developed.

FIGURE 9
Aerial view of the Getty Villa under construction, May 1972. Photo: JPGM Archives

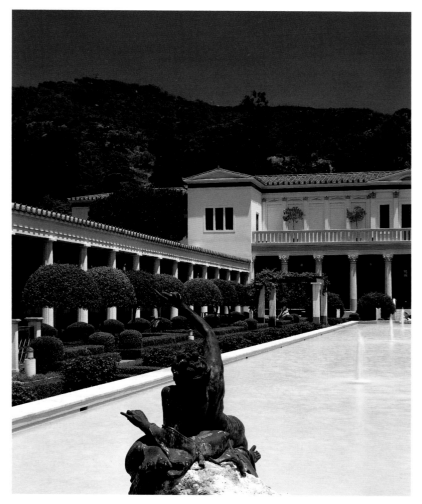

FIGURE 10
View of the Getty Villa Museum from Main Peristyle Garden. Photo: Alexander Vertikoff

At his death in June 1976, Getty bequeathed four million shares of
Getty Oil stock, worth about $700 million, to his Museum, leaving it to
the trustees' discretion to decide how the legacy should best be used. Although the assets would be tied up in the courts for some time to come,
the collections grew impressively in the first years after he died through the
receipt of Getty's private collection from Sutton Place and purchases made
with income from the estate. Significant acquisitions included the late fourth-
century-B.C. Greek bronze statue of Victorious Youth (see pp. 32–33), the
Saint Andrew by Masaccio (see p. 93), and the Corner Cupboard by Jacques
Dubois (see pp. 208–209).

Early in 1981 the trustees appointed Harold M. Williams, chairman of the Securities and Exchange Commission during the Carter administration, to be president and chief executive officer of the J. Paul Getty Trust. By April 1982, with the receipt of the proceeds of Getty's estate, the Trust already had begun to prepare for its transformation from a small museum into a visual arts institution of international significance. Realizing that the new income represented an unparalleled opportunity to expand upon Getty's initial vision, Williams and the trustees moved to set up other organizations that could operate in tandem with the Getty Museum in furtherance of J. Paul Getty's mandate for "the diffusion of artistic and general knowledge." They created new programs dedicated to advanced scholarship in the arts and humanities, an expanded art library, conservation and cultural heritage preservation, visual arts education in primary and secondary schools, and the use of computer technology to improve access to art and humanities information. They also established a grant program supporting a range of projects and publications across the entire spectrum of interests of the Getty Trust.

Income from Getty's legacy would permit the Museum to expand its collections dramatically. This possibility, and the space requirements of the new programs of the Trust, suggested that a new building be built somewhere else, allowing the original building in Malibu to house the Museum's antiquities collection. Williams and the trustees envisioned a complex similar to a university campus where all the Getty organizations would be gathered together, a place where the many approaches to art—display, scholarship, conservation, education—could flourish, and where new forms of collaboration would come naturally. A dramatic, 750-acre spur of the Santa Monica Mountains in west Los Angeles was purchased in 1983 and plans for the Getty Center were set in motion. John Walsh, who had been a paintings curator at the Metropolitan Museum of Art and the Museum of Fine Arts, Boston, as well as a university professor, became the director of the Getty Museum in 1983. In October 1984, after a lengthy selection process, the trustees named Richard Meier of New York the project architect.

The Getty Center, whose construction began in 1989 after six years of planning, became the largest single-phase building project in the history of Los Angeles (fig. 11), with more than a thousand people working on the site. It opened to the public in December 1997. More than four and a half million people have already visited the Center. Harold Williams, the Getty's president and chief executive for seventeen years, retired in January 1998, just weeks after the official opening. He was succeeded by Barry Munitz, former chancellor of the California State University system, who,

FIGURE 11

View of the arrival plaza and the Getty Museum at the Getty Center, looking south.
Photo: John Edward Linden

together with the Board of Trustees, quickly set about refining the Getty's
mission. As this *Handbook* is being edited, the Getty has embarked on a
number of exciting changes under Munitz's leadership. Institutes have been
reorganized and some activities internally shifted; the organization is
actively pursuing the opportunities for partnerships as well as for leadership
that the visibility of the Getty Center has brought.

While the Center is a world apart from the verdant canyon of the
Museum in Malibu, it was planned to provide visitors many of the same pleasures, especially the memorable experience of buildings and gardens,
courtyards and views. Meier's design takes full advantage of the pleasures
provided by the site in the Santa Monica mountains, and it reveals his
deep interest in light and geometry. Works of art are well served in Meier's
galleries, which are proportioned and lighted for the pieces they contain
and arranged in a more lucid sequence than was the case in Malibu. Entire
collections that had been shoehorned into confined spaces or shown only
in part finally have ample room.

Natural daylight, almost entirely absent from the galleries in Malibu,
is abundant, both for paintings and for changing exhibitions, for which
a special pavilion was built. Recognizing that visitors better enjoy and re-
member works of art for which they are given information, art information
rooms have been provided among the galleries where they can learn about
objects and their contexts in a variety of ways, including participatory
activities guided by staff and docents, and electronic media.

As this revised *Handbook of the Collections* is being printed, a selection
of the Getty Museum's Greek, Roman, and Etruscan antiquities collection

FIGURE 12
Artist's rendering of renovated skylight gallery at the Villa, prepared by Machado and Silvetti Associates, Inc.

is on display temporarily at the Getty Center. In the near future, these collections will return to the renovated Villa and gardens in Malibu (fig. 12), which will welcome visitors to a world of discoveries. Suitably redesigned galleries will display more of the Museum's extensive collections of antiquities than ever before, and temporary exhibition spaces will allow the presentation of loan shows. The Villa will have a more complex and exciting mission than previously to awaken the public to the fascination, as well as the contemporary relevance, of the arts and cultures of antiquity; to foster the study of the Classical world and its relation to other cultures; and to train young professionals to care for artifacts and sites around the world. A library, seminar facilities, and offices for scholars will support research programs. A complex of laboratories will accommodate both the Museum's Antiquities Conservation Department and a new graduate degree program for conservation of archaeological and ethnographic materials offered in collaboration with the University of California, Los Angeles. New facilities will also support a varied menu of public programs including lectures, concerts, and theatrical performances.

For those who work at the Getty Center, and for those preparing to reopen the Getty Villa, J. Paul Getty's legacy has brought the professional adventure of a lifetime. For the Museum's visitors it will go on furnishing new surprises, pleasure, and rewards.

N.B.
Getty's own observations as quoted here have been taken from the following books written by or with him: *Collector's Choice* (with Ethel Le Vane), London: W. H. Allen, 1955; *The Joys of Collecting*, New York: Hawthorn Books, 1965; and *As I See It*, Englewood Cliffs: Prentice-Hall, 1976.

Antiquities

The Museum's antiquities collection began with J. Paul Getty's purchase of a small Classical terracotta sculpture at a Sotheby's auction in London in 1939. The thirty-eight years that passed between that time and Getty's last direct acquisition, a marble head of a Roman youth, witnessed the creation of a collection of ancient Greek and Roman art that was the third most important of its kind in the United States.

For many years the collection's greatest strength was in sculpture. It was the heart of the antiquities collection when Getty was alive, and many of the Museum's most interesting examples of ancient sculpture, including the dedicatory group with a portrait of Alexander the Great (see p. 23) and the Tarentine terracotta group of a seated poet and sirens (see p. 43), were acquired under Getty's personal direction.

In the years since his death, the collection has continued to grow. Several major acquisitions of Greek sculpture have been made, including the Victorious Youth (see pp. 32 – 33) and the brilliantly painted group composed of two griffins attacking a fallen doe (see p. 20). Other additions have included a number of Cycladic marble sculptures of the Aegean Bronze Age (see pp. 17 – 18) and the Cult Statue of a Goddess from the Classical period (see pp. 20 – 21).

Important acquisitions have also been made in other areas; the collection of vases has grown to be the department's strongest holding. Included are such masterpieces as the kylix painted by Douris and the "Chalcidian" amphora attributed to the Inscription Painter (see pp. 49 and 46). Other noteworthy acquisitions have been made in the areas of Roman bronze sculpture, Greek and Roman gems, and such luxury wares as Hellenistic silver and Roman glass. The most recent and substantial addition has been the important collection of Lawrence and Barbara Fleischman, consisting of some three hundred objects made in a variety of media and ranging in date from the Bronze Age to late antiquity. Outstanding for their rarity and excellent state of preservation are the Cycladic Head of a Figure (see p. 17) and the bronze Lebes (see p. 33). While the scope of the Museum's collection has been extended to include fine examples of Romano-Egyptian portrait painting and cast bronzes from Northern Europe, its focus has been and will continue to be art of the Classical period.

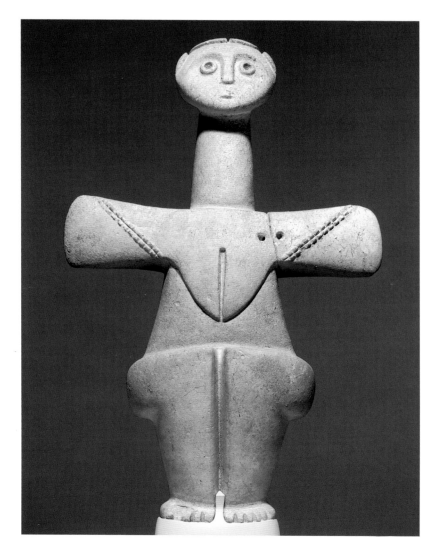

FERTILITY GODDESS

Cypriot, 3000 – 2500 B.C.
Limestone
42.4 × 27.7 cm
(16½ × 10¹¹⁄₁₆ in.)
83.AA.38

Cypriot female figurines are among the earliest sculpted objects of artistic importance from the eastern Mediterranean area. Since they usually range in height from only about an inch to just over a foot, the Museum's statuette is one of the largest known. With head raised, arms extended, and legs drawn up, this figure appears to be squatting, perhaps giving birth. The phallic character of the head and neck is intentional, and the configuration of the breasts implies female genitalia. The holes drilled in the figure's left shoulder and arm are part of an ancient repair: the broken arm was fastened on by a cord threaded through the holes. Such careful treatment proves that this statuette was prized by its ancient owner.

HEAD OF A FIGURE OF THE EARLY SPEDOS TYPE

Early Cycladic,
2600–2500 B.C.
Island marble with
polychromy
22.8 × 8.9 cm (9 × 3½ in.)
96.AA.27

Although this head from a Cycladic figure is rare in that it is almost life-size, its features follow the abstract simplicity that is typical of Cycladic statues. This piece is also important in that it preserves much of the colorful detailing that most likely decorated all Cycladic sculpture: a fringe of hair across the brow, dotted tattooing on the cheekbones, and a stripe along the bridge of the nose. These finely carved and modern-looking statuettes were created in the Bronze Age (circa 3000–1100 B.C.) and have been found throughout the eastern Mediterranean.

HARPIST

Early Cycladic II,
circa 2500 B.C.
Island marble
35.8 × 9.5 cm (14 × 3¹¹/₁₆ in.)
85.AA.103

Men are infrequently represented in Cycladic art. When they do appear, they are often musicians who play the harp or a wind instrument. This seated harpist is the sole male Cycladic figurine in the Museum's collection, and one of only ten harpists known today. He sits on a four-legged stool, his left hand encircling the frame of his instrument and his right hand resting on its sound box. The original purpose of the figure is unknown. Such figures may have been created as protective idols that accompanied their owners to the grave.

FEMALE FIGURE OF THE LATE SPEDOS TYPE

Attributed to the
Steiner Master
Early Cycladic II,
2500 – 2400 B.C.
Island marble
H: 59.9 cm (23⅝ in.)
88.AA.80

Discovered on the Greek islands known as the Cyclades, female figures of this kind have been found in both burial sites and sanctuaries, although their exact purpose remains unknown. This piece belongs to the best-known and most numerous figure type, those reclining with folded arms. The details of the human body are reduced to a minimum, and the figure is a flattened, schematic representation that approaches pure abstraction. Incision delineates the arms from the body, separates the thighs, and defines the abdomen and pubic triangle. Many statuettes originally were enhanced with brightly colored pigments that accentuated anatomical features and decorative markings.

SLAB WITH RELIEF OF A YOUNG HUNTER

Greek (Macedonia),
350 – 300 B.C.
Marble
143.1 × 42.7 cm
(56⅜ × 16¹¹/₁₆ in.)
96.AA.48

A young hunter is shown in relief with his spears propped on his shoulder. Slung from the weapons is an indistinct object, possibly a traveling hat or a net bag for holding the day's catch. Since the relief was originally painted, colored details would have helped to identify the item. The architectural molding preserved at the top right edge of the slab confirms that it formed the right-hand wall of a three-sided funerary shrine (*naiskos*). The figure of the hunter would have looked toward an image of the deceased on the back wall.

Grave Stele of the Hoplite Pollis

Greek (probably from
Megara), circa 480 B.C.
Marble
149.8 × 44.5 cm
(58⁷⁄₁₆ × 17⅛ in.)
90.AA.129

The style of this figure displays innovations in the rendering of human anatomy and perspective made during the Early Classical period (480 – 450 B.C.). The body is defined with confident, sharp contours, the surfaces of the musculature are accurately carved with subtly modeled anatomical details, the profile pose is nearly correctly rendered, and the warrior appears as if he were about to move. His angled shield is sculpted to show its deep interior curve. Made to mark the grave of a Greek foot soldier (hoplite) named Pollis, this stele probably stood in or near the Greek city-state of Megara, midway between Athens and Corinth. The three-line inscription written in Megarian script above the figure of Pollis reads: "I speak, Pollis, the beloved son of Asopitos, having not died a coward [but fighting] in the line of battle." The nude Pollis is armed with a spear in his right hand, a round shield on his left arm, a sword at his left side, and a helmet. This monument to a brave warrior was made around the time that the Greeks were fighting the Persians in 480 B.C.

SCULPTURAL GROUP OF TWO GRIFFINS ATTACKING A FALLEN DOE

Greek (South Italy), late
fourth century B.C.
Marble with polychromy
95 × 148 cm (37⅟₁₆ × 57¼ in.)
85.AA.106

The surviving pigments on this sculptural group provide a vivid reminder that all ancient marbles were
once brightly painted. In a remarkable feat of sculpting,
the artist has captured the notion of dangerous beauty
by juxtaposing the lithe, sinuous forms of the griffins
with the brutality of their attack on the ill-fated doe.
The symmetrical, upright, sickle-shaped wings were
functionally necessary, for the channels carved between
the wings indicate that the piece served as a support,
probably for a ceremonial table.

CULT STATUE OF A GODDESS, PERHAPS APHRODITE

Greek (South Italy),
425 – 400 B.C.
Limestone and Parian
marble with polychromy
H: 220 cm (85¹³⁄₁₆ in.)
88.AA.76

The over-life-size proportions, quality of execution,
and the fact that the figure is finished on all sides suggest that this statue was made as a cult image, or
sacred representation of the deity, intended to stand
within a temple. The voluptuous proportions of the
figure and the carefully articulated suggestion of
breezes moving the drapery make it most likely that
the subject is Aphrodite, the goddess of love and sexuality. It is sculpted from an unusual combination of
materials: fine limestone is used for the draped body
and Parian marble is used for the head, preserved
arm, and foot. Although this statue is surely a product
of the Greek colonies of South Italy and Sicily, it
nevertheless strongly reflects the style of Late Classical
sculpture from Athens.

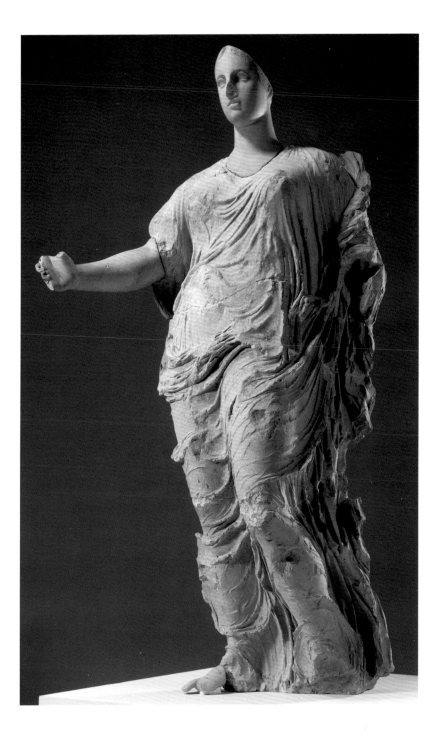

LEKANIS

Greek (South Italy),
late fourth century B.C.
Marble with polychromy
H: 30.8 cm (12 in.);
DIAM: 60 cm (23¼ in.)
85.AA.107

The decoration on the interior of this unique ceremonial basin provides a sense of the original appearance of Greek wall painting. Rendered in vivid polychromy, Thetis and two Nereids ride to the left, one on a spirited sea horse (*hippocampos*), the other two on sea monsters (*kete*). Each carries a piece of armor for Thetis's son Achilles, the greatest Greek hero in the Trojan War. When the lekanis was filled with water, the illusion that the Nereids were riding over the sea would have been complete. The basin was probably used for a foot-washing ritual.

PORTRAIT OF A BEARDED MAN

Greek, Hellenistic,
160 – 150 B.C.
Marble
40.7 × 25 cm (16¹⁄₁₆ × 9⅞ in.)
91.AA.14

Although the size and individualized features indicate that this head is a portrait of an important man, the lack of a diadem signifies that he was not a king at the time it was carved. Stylistically the head relates closely to the figures of gods and goddesses fighting giants on the Great Altar of Zeus at Pergamon, a city on the western coast of Turkey, and to other Pergamene portraits. The subject may have been a high-ranking member of the powerful Attalid dynasty that ruled Pergamon during the Hellenistic period (323 – 31 B.C.), possibly Attalos II. The head was once part of a draped standing sculpture; traces of a mantle remain on the back of the neck. The head was damaged in antiquity and has survived as two large fragments.

Portrait of Alexander the Great

Greek, circa 320 B.C.
Marble
H: 28 cm (10¹⁵⁄₁₆ in.)
73.AA.27

Identifiable by the manelike, swept-back hair and the deep-set, upturned eyes, this head is undoubtedly a portrait of Alexander the Great (356–323 B.C.). This portrait type of the youthful conqueror of the Persian Empire and India was created by Lysippos, the only sculptor Alexander allowed to portray him during his short life. It combines elements of Alexander's actual appearance with features of ideal representations of gods and heroes. The head belongs to a statue that probably was part of a commemorative monument composed of several figures, including Alexander's favorite companion, Hephaestion.

STATUE OF
TYCHE

Greek, Hellenistic,
150 – 100 B.C.
Island marble
H: 84.5 cm (33¼ in.)
96.AA.49

Tyche, the personification of a specific city and, more generally, the goddess of good fortune, is identified by her turreted mural crown. During the Hellenistic period (323 – 31 B.C.), when many cities were being founded by Alexander the Great's successors, large statues of Tyche were commissioned to ensure safety and prosperity. Smaller statues of Tyche, such as this one, were most likely adaptations of the life-size or colossal public representations. This statue was originally adorned with real earrings and a necklace, secured through holes in her ears and veil. Other details would have been added with paint.

PORTRAIT OF CALIGULA

Roman, A.D. 37–41
Marble
H: 43 cm (16¼ in.)
72.AA.155

Gaius Julius Caesar Germanicus, the third emperor of Rome (reigned A.D. 37–41), spent his early childhood in a Roman army camp in Germany. Since his parents dressed him in a military costume that included *caligae*, the footgear of a soldier, the legionnaires gave him the nickname Caligula, or Little Boots. He became Emperor of Rome at the age of twenty-five but was assassinated within four years because his reign had turned despotic and his behavior, cruelly erratic. Because of his unpopularity, most portraits of Caligula were destroyed after his death. This surviving likeness reflects Julio-Claudian classicism.

PORTRAIT BUST OF A ROMAN LADY

Roman, A.D. 150–160
Carrara marble
H: 67.5 cm (26⁹⁄₁₆ in.)
83.AA.44

The features of this elegant lady convey a placid yet intriguing character. Although her face is unlined, she is no longer young; one detects the confident self-assurance of a Roman matron secure in her status. Her elaborate coiffure is in the fashion of Faustina the Elder, wife of Emperor Antoninus Pius (reigned A.D. 138–161), and the high polish also dates the piece to the Antonine period. This bust provides a fine example of the unique achievement of the Roman portrait sculptors.

LANSDOWNE HERAKLES

Roman copy after a Greek
original of 375 – 350 B.C.
by the Polykleitan school,
circa A.D. 125
Pentelic marble
H: 193.5 cm (76⁹⁄₁₆ in.)
70.AA.109

As an exemplar of human achievement and the subject of philosophical discussion, Herakles was an appropriate model for a Roman emperor. This statue was
found at Tivoli in 1790 or 1791 in the ruins of the
villa of the emperor Hadrian (reigned A.D. 117 – 138).
Until 1951 it was in the collection of the marquess
of Lansdowne. The Lansdowne Herakles was one of
J. Paul Getty's favorite pieces. The young Herakles is
shown larger than life-size, carrying the club with
which he slew the Nemean lion and holding its skin.

SARCOPHAGUS WITH LID

Roman (Athens),
late second–early third
century A.D.
Pentelic marble
Box: 134 × 147 × 249 cm
(53 × 58 × 98 in.)
Lid: 100 × 95 × 218 cm
(39⅜ × 37⅜ × 86 in.)
95.AA.80

Carved in high relief on three sides of the box are
scenes from the legend of Achilles, the Greek hero of
the Trojan War and a central figure in Homer's *Iliad*.
On the right end, Achilles is discovered by Odysseus
hiding among the daughters of King Lykomedes
on the island of Skyros to avoid joining the Greeks at
Troy. On the left end, Achilles arms for battle with
Odysseus and a spear carrier (*doryphoros*) looking on.
The armor he dons is new, recently received from
his mother, the Nereid Thetis. The result of Achilles'
confrontation with the great Trojan hero Hektor is
shown on the front, as Achilles mounts his chariot to
drag Hektor's body around the walls of the city. On
the back of the sarcophagus the shallower relief scene
of Lapiths fighting Centaurs may also be understood
as a reference to Achilles, who was educated by the
Centaur Chiron. On the lid two figures recline on an
elaborate couch. Their heads were left in an unfin-
ished state so that the portraits of the deceased could
be carved after the piece was purchased.

Portrait of a Balding Man

Roman (Asia Minor),
circa A.D. 240
Proconessian marble
H: 25.5 cm (10 in.)
85.AA.112

This beautifully carved and well-preserved portrait head depicts a balding, elderly man. The individualized features suggest that he may have been a person of some importance. The fact that the striking blue-gray marble from which the portrait is carved comes from the area around the island of Marmara in modern-day Turkey may indicate that the subject was a Roman citizen of Asia Minor. The unknown artist skillfully utilized the contrasting techniques of deep drill work and high polish to differentiate between the textures of the subject's smooth skin and tightly curled hair.

Statuette of a Seated Lion

Greek (Lakonia),
mid-sixth century B.C.
Bronze
9.3 × 5 × 13. 3 cm
(3⅝ × 1¹⁵⁄₁₆ × 5¼ in.)
96.AB.76

Serving a decorative or dedicatory function, this hollow-cast bronze statuette of a lion is seated in an alert pose, emphasized by its upright ears, arched eyebrows, and bulging eyes. Like other representations of lions manufactured in Lakonia, the region around the ancient city of Sparta in southern Greece, this one has an incised mane and mild demeanor.

FURNITURE
SUPPORT
REPRESENTING A
WINGED FELINE

Tartessian, 700 – 575 B.C.
Bronze with gilding
H: 61 cm (24 in.)
79.AB.140

Although winged felines were popular
in Greek, Phoenician, and Assyrian art,
this creature's articulated wings and
curved brow point to an origin in
Tartessos, the Phoenician colony on
the southwest coast of the Iberian penin-
sula. The beast was cast in two separate
pieces that are joined with rivets just
below the wings. The thin bronze rods
between the head and wings could
be design features, but more likely they
are part of the bronze mold's internal
system of tubes, which facilitated the
flow of the molten metal. The pierced
projections behind the head and below
the front paws of the winged creature
indicate that it was attached to a larger
structure, such as a wooden throne.

STATUETTE OF
A RIDER

Greek (Corinth),
circa 550 B.C.
Bronze
H: 8.5 cm (3⅛ in.)
96.AB.45

Filled with youthful exuberance, this
small figure once sat astride a large
horse, his muscular legs tensely clinging
to the sides of the mount. The top of
his head is flattened, suggesting that he
originally wore a hat. He may be one of
the Dioskouroi, the twin sons of Zeus,
who were renowned horsemen. A similar bronze was found at the sanctuary
of Zeus in Dodona, in northern Greece.
The object most likely served as a
votive offering, which would have been
dedicated at a sanctuary.

STATUETTE OF A FALLEN YOUTH

Greek, 480–460 B.C.
Bronze with copper inlays
7.3 × 13.5 cm (2⅞ × 5¼ in.)
86.AB.530

The closed eyes, prostrate pose, and twisted torso of this figure suggest that he is likely dead. He may be a fallen warrior holding his weapons (now missing) who was part of a group composition, perhaps showing figures in a landscape. The beautifully articulated details of this figure are the work of a master craftsman. Copper inlays were used for curls of the hair and the nipples. These inlays, now lost or altered by oxidation and burial, once created a rich contrast with the golden tones of the figure's polished bronze flesh.

STATUETTE OF A BEARDED MAN

Etruscan (Piombino),
circa 480 B.C.
Bronze
H: 17.2 cm (6¹¹⁄₁₆ in.)
55.AB.12

Said to have been found in Piombino, this figure is a fine example of Early Classical Etruscan statuary. The rigid frontality of its pose and the advanced left leg are vestiges of the earlier Archaic style, but the more naturalistic treatment of the torso and face are new. The figure wears a *tebenna*, the Etruscan precursor of the Roman toga. Perhaps the now-missing object he held in his clenched left hand was a scepter, justifying his frequent identification as Tinia, the Etruscan equivalent of the king of the Greek gods, Zeus.

Portrait of a Man

Roman (Asia Minor),
first century B.C.
Bronze
H: 29.5 cm (11½ in.)
73.AB.8

This head, which once had realistic inlaid eyes and lips inlaid with copper, was part of a full-length statue. The image is a powerful and vigorous one, befitting a Hellenistic leader. It may represent the Roman general Sulla (138–78 B.C.), who waged ruthless campaigns in Greece and Asia Minor, where this portrait is said to have been found. It shows the idealized features characteristic of portraits of men whose rule was legitimized by courage and will rather than by divine or royal status.

Statuette of an Old Woman

Greek, Late Hellenistic,
first century B.C.
Bronze
H: 12.6 cm (4¹⁵⁄₁₆ in.)
96.AB.175

Although the objects once held in her hands are now missing, the pose of this frail old woman suggests that she is spinning wool. She would have held a distaff with raw wool in her left hand and twisted the thread away from her body with her right hand. She tilts her head downward, following the movement of the thread. Her clothing is reflective of the humble attire worn by women engaged in domestic and agricultural tasks. Representing people of varying ages and status in a variety of poses was of great interest during the Hellenistic period (323–30 B.C.).

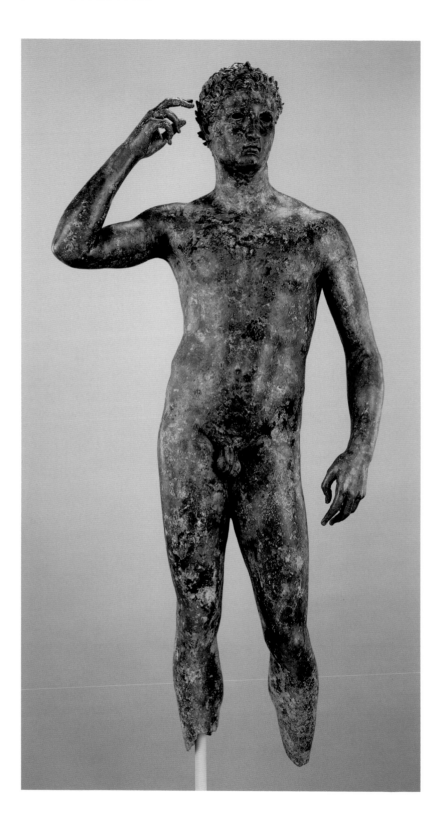

Statue of a Victorious Youth

Greek, 325 – 300 B.C.
Bronze with copper inlays
H: 151.5 cm (59⅝ in.)
77.AB.30

Few monumental Greek bronze sculptures have survived. Among them, this representation of a victorious young man is one of the finest examples from the last decades of the fourth century. Standing confidently, the subject raises his right hand beside his head, on which he has just placed the olive wreath of victory. Each city or sanctuary that hosted competitions awarded wreaths made from a specific plant to their winners, and the olive wreath was the prize given to the victor in the most prestigious of all of these contests, at Olympia. This sculpture most likely was dedicated there.

The artist is unknown, but the figure's open stance, the small size of the head relative to the body, and the slight torsion of the pose strongly reflect the innovations of Lysippos, the fourth-century-B.C. sculptor who specialized in cast-bronze figures.

Lebes

Greek, Late Hellenistic,
50 – 1 B.C.
Bronze with silver inlays
H: 58 cm (22¹¹⁄₁₆ in.)
96.AC.51

Adorning the front of this cauldron, or *lebes*, is a half-length figure of a young satyr, a member of the retinue of Dionysos, the god of wine. The handsome rustic snaps his fingers and bares his teeth in a wild, impudent grin; his eyes and teeth are silvered. This figure and the large grape leaf below the handle in the back imply that the object functioned in some aspect of the Dionysiac cult, possibly for serving wine. The good condition of this piece suggests that it may have been placed in a tomb, either as an urn or a funerary offering.

HERM OF
DIONYSOS

Attributed to the
Workshop of Boethos
Greek, Late Hellenistic,
100 – 50 B.C.
Bronze with ivory inlay
H: 103.5 cm (40⅞ in.);
W (base): 23.5 cm (9⅛ in.)
79.AB.138

In Greece and Rome, a sculpture called
a herm was a rectangular pillar surmounted by a head, often of Hermes, the
god of travelers, commerce, and thieves.
Herms stood at crossroads to protect
travelers and at the entrances of homes
to keep evil away. The Getty herm is
unusual in featuring a bearded, turbaned
image of Dionysos, the god of wine
and the theater. In common with other
large-scale Greek bronzes, the head
had inlaid ivory eyes with the iris and
pupil added in colored stone. One ivory
eye remains, and the bronze eyelashes
are also visible. This herm is very
similar to one that was discovered with
other Greek bronze sculptures in an
ancient shipwreck off Mahdia on the
coast of Tunisia. The two herms appear
to be two different versions of a single
original model. The Mahdia herm
was signed by the sculptor Boethos
of Kalchedon, whose works were highly
prized by Roman collectors of Greek art.

MINIATURE PORTRAIT BUST OF A YOUNG WOMAN

Roman, late first century B.C.
Bronze with glass-paste inlays
H: 16.5 cm (6⁷⁄₁₆ in.)
84.AB.59

Remarkably detailed and well preserved, this small bust of a Roman lady attests to the sensitivity of the craftsman responsible for its manufacture. After casting, the head was engraved with many details, in particular with the braided and knotted hairstyle popular during the reign of Augustus (31 B.C.–A.D. 14). The earrings are missing; but the inlaid eyes of glass paste, which do not usually survive from antiquity, are preserved and add to the head's strikingly realistic impression.

PORTRAIT BUST OF MENANDER

Roman, early
first century A.D.
Bronze
H: 17 cm (6⅝ in.)
72.AB.108

The faint inscription (MENANΔ PO( ) on the round base of this bust identifies this man as the Greek playwright Menander (342/41 – 291/90 B.C.). His comic plays were famous in his own time, and later they were adapted by Latin authors such as Plautus and Terence for Roman audiences. Although many replicas of this portrait type exist, this bust is one of two known versions inscribed with Menander's name, confirming the identity of this popular image.

THYMIATERION

Roman, first half of
the first century A.D.
Bronze with silver inlays
H: 23.3 cm (9⅛ in.)
87.AC.143

This incense burner features an actor
who wears the clothing and mask associated with productions of Greek New
Comedy. The mask's wide open mouth
was appropriate for comic effect and the
amplification of speech. The figure is
hollow, however, and the altar on which
he sits is pierced underneath for venti-
lation. As the incense smoldered inside
the altar, the perfumed smoke would
emerge through the actor's open mouth.

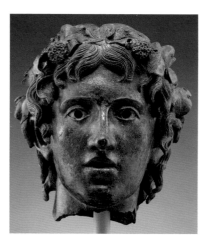

HEAD OF THE
YOUNG DIONYSOS

Roman, A.D. 1–50
Bronze with silver inlays
H: 21.6 cm (8½ in.)
96.AB.52

The twisted vine wreath covered with
leaves and berries indicates that this
life-size head is that of Dionysos, the
god of wine, represented here as a beautiful youth. The pupils and irises of
his eyes would have been inlaid in glass
or stone, making him appear very life-
like. Despite these missing elements,
the dreamy expression still verges on the
erotic, with an intent to transfix recep-
tive viewers. Judging from similar
statues of a youthful Dionysos, this head
was once part of a full-length figure
that might have served as a lamp or tray
bearer.

STATUETTE OF CERES OR JUNO

Roman, A.D. 40–68
Bronze
H: 32 cm (12½ in.)
84.AB.670

Clad in a long tunic and mantle, this figure is identified as a deity by her diadem. Her original attributes are missing, but the positioning of her hands suggests that she held an offering dish (*patera*) in her right one and a scepter or spear in her left. While various Roman goddesses are represented with these attributes on coins of the period, this figure is probably either Ceres (the Greek Demeter) or Juno (the Greek Hera). A large, square hole in the back of the statuette indicates that it was once fastened to another object, perhaps a chariot or a piece of furniture.

STATUETTE OF ROMA OR VIRTUS

Roman, A.D. 40–68
Bronze
H: 33.1 cm (12¹⁵⁄₁₆ in.)
84.AB.671

The impact of Greek classicism on Roman imperial art is evident in this fine statuette of a female deity. The figurine once held objects that established her identity. She might represent Roma, the personification of the city and empire of Rome, or Virtus, the embodiment of valor. Common to both are the helmet, spear, and short chiton, or dress, that leaves the right breast bared. The distinguishing attribute would have been held in her right hand: a winged Victory if Roma or a sword if Virtus. This figure may have been part of a group that included the bronze Statuette of Ceres or Juno (see previous entry) and the Togate Magistrates (see p. 38).

RELIEF WITH TWO TOGATE MAGISTRATES

Roman, A.D. 40–68
Bronze
26 × 13.8 cm (10⅛ × 5⅜ in.)
85.AB.109

The togas worn by these men identify them as members of the upper classes. The older wears the shoes of a senator and holds a scroll in his left hand, indicating that he is either a priest or a local official. The shoe of the younger man is that of a knight. These figures are hollow on the back and, along with the Museum's statuettes of Roma or Virtus and Ceres or Juno (see p. 37), probably formed part of the decoration of a ceremonial chariot or a large piece of furniture.

ARYBALLOS

Roman (Gaul), A.D. 70–100
Bronze with red and blue champlevé enamel
H: 10.5 cm (4⅛ in.)
96.AC.190

The round shape and flaring mouth of this aryballos recall the features of terracotta oil containers made in ancient Greece. Two large rings, which pass through elephant-head lugs on either side of the rim, fit over the ends of the handle. Enamel inlays ornament the five-sided panels that decorate the body. Within these panels are curling tendrils enframing smaller pentagons that contain either the image of a bird or a rosette. The use of enamel is typical of vessels produced in the northern part of the Roman province of Gaul.

PAIR OF PORTRAIT BUSTS

Roman (Gaul), A.D. 60–70
Bronze
H(.1): 40.6 cm (15 ¹¹/₁₆ in.);
H(.2): 40 cm (15 ⅝ in.)
89.AB.67.1–.2

These two hollow-cast busts were made from the same mold, and only minor differences in appearance distinguish them from one another. Their empty eye sockets were originally inlaid with realistic eyes crafted from colored materials. Their distinctive hairstyle with the wave across the forehead was common in the reign of the Roman emperor Nero (A.D. 54–68). Long, separately made strands of hair were once attached to the backs of their heads, a hairstyle associated with boys who served as sacrificial attendants (*camilli*) for various Roman cults or were special attendants (*tirones*) in an imperial youth organization known as the *Iuventus* (Latin for "the youth" or "young men"). The intended purpose of the *Iuventus* was to prepare aristocratic young men of Rome and its provinces for military service and later for governmental posts. Under Nero it also formed an imperial honor guard. The style of the busts suggests that they were created in Gaul, where they would most likely have been displayed in a local shrine of the *Iuventus*.

STATUETTE OF MARS / COBANNUS

Roman (Gaul),
A.D. 125 – 175
Bronze
H: 76 cm (29¹⁵⁄₁₆ in.)
96.AB.54

The Latin inscription on its base identifies this figure as Cobannus, a local Gallic god identified with Mars, the Roman god of war: "Sacred to the venerable god Cobannus, Lucius Maccius Aeternus, *duumvir*, [dedicated this] in accordance with a vow." In style, the sculpture is a distinctly Gallo-Roman creation. Instead of the customary image of Mars as a mature, bearded man, the god appears here as an idealized youth who wears a contemporary Roman legionary helmet. His costume — a long-sleeved tunic and long leggings worn under a Greek-style cloak — is typical of northern provincial dress. The dedicator of this statue, Lucius Maccius Aeternus, was a *duumvir*, one of the two chief magistrates of a Roman colony.

SITULA

Roman (probably Asia
Minor), A.D. 220–320
Bronze with tin plating
H: 33.5 cm (13¾₆ in.);
DIAM (rim): 27.2 cm
(10¹¹⁄₁₆ in.)
96.AC.55

This elegant slender vessel once had a
swinging handle and served as a situla,
or bucket. Its shape goes back to that of
the Greek *kalathos*, a tall flaring basket.
These types of baskets had many uses,
but were especially associated with wool
working and the harvest. On the main
frieze of this container is a lively Dionysiac procession, particularly appropriate
if this were used in conjunction with the
grape harvest. The god of wine reclines
on a chariot that is drawn by felines.
Riding the felines is Eros, who holds up
bunches of grapes. In front of Dionysos,
a nude young satyr, one of Dionysos's
retinue, runs on tiptoe. Behind Dionysos's chariot are a dancing maenad,
a goat-legged Pan, and old Silenos, also
members of Dionysos's circle.

ANTEFIX IN THE FORM OF A MAENAD AND SATYR DANCING

South Etruscan,
early fifth century B.C.
Terracotta
H: 54.6 cm (21½ in.)
96.AD.33

Once decorating the edge of a roof
of an Etruscan temple or civic building,
this figural group was made from a
mold. The maenad, who holds castanets
(*krotola*) in her right hand, seems to
turn her head away from the amorous
satyr, who eagerly embraces her. He
holds a drinking horn in his left hand,
which adds a sense of revelry. The
original pigments are exceptionally
well preserved and serve as a reminder
that most ancient sculpture and much
of the architecture was brightly painted.

Pair of Altars

Greek (probably Taranto),
400 – 375 B.C.
Terracotta
41.8 × 31.5 cm
(16⅜ × 12⅜ in.)
86.AD.598.1 – .2

The imagery on these two altars forms one composition. On the right altar, Aphrodite, the goddess of love and sexuality, and her lover Adonis, associated with vegetation and fertility, sit side-by-side in a rocky landscape. Adonis puts his right arm around the goddess. Two women attend them, one standing and carrying a drum, the other seated in a pose associated with mourning. On the left altar, three women dance toward the lovers; two carry musical instruments, a drum and a xylophone. These scenes emphasize the sadness and joy of the myth of Adonis who, like a plant, was fated to die and be reborn each year. Probably made for a private shrine, these small altars were used for the burning of offerings or incense.

Seated Poet and Sirens

Greek (probably Taranto),
circa 310 B.C.
Terracotta with polychromy
Poet H: 104 cm (40⅞ in.);
Sirens H: 140 cm (54⅝ in.)
76.AD.11.1 – .3

Once brightly painted, this trio of large clay figures has often been identified as Orpheus and the Sirens. Orpheus was a mythical singer, or poet, who survived a journey to the realm of the dead, and sirens were monstrous bird-women known for their sweet and seductive song, which enraptured and drew sailors to their deaths. Here, the seated man is singing, as shown by his open mouth and the object in his right hand, which is the handle of the pick (*plektron*) used to strike the strings of a harp (*kithara*). His instrument, now entirely missing, once rested in the hollow on his lap.

Because he is singing and playing the harp, the seated figure has been identified as Orpheus; his attire, however, does not match what is found in many contemporary representations of the poet. On fourth-century-B.C. Apulian vases Orpheus is usually shown in an elaborately embroidered oriental costume — a long, flowing robe with a short, capelike chlamys around the shoulders — and a soft Phrygian cap. Since sirens, as figures who mourn the dead and help fulfill the promise of life after death, are often found in a funerary context, the seated man may be a simple mortal, depicted as a poet.

OINOCHOE

East Greek (Rhodes),
circa 625 B.C.
Terracotta
H: 35.7 cm (14 in.);
DIAM (body): 26.5 cm
(10⁷⁄₁₆ in.)
81.AE.83

This trefoil *oinochoe*, or pitcher with a
three-lobed spout, is decorated in a
black-on-white style of vase painting
characteristic of the Orientalizing
period of the seventh century B.C. This
particular type of painting first appeared
on Greek ceramics made in Asia Minor.
The Rhodian variety is painted in the
Wild Goat style, named after its most
common motif. Borrowed from the arts
of the ancient Near East, the decorative
elements of the style remained largely
unchanged for nearly a century. Here the
figural subjects are exclusively animals,
real and imaginary, with floral and geometric patterns used as filler ornaments
and framing borders.

ARYBALLOS

Greek (Corinth), first quarter
of sixth century B.C.
Terracotta
H: 11.2 cm (4⅜ in.);
DIAM: 11.7 cm (4⁹⁄₁₆ in.)
92.AE.4

A rare example of narrative art produced
in the city of Corinth, this oil container
depicts Herakles battling the serpentine
Hydra. He thrusts his sword toward
the Hydra's weaving heads in an attempt
to chop them off but is bitten on the
shoulder by one of them. Behind Herakles stands Athena, his patron goddess.
To the right, Herakles' nephew Iolaos
helps to defeat the monster. The names
of Athena, Herakles, and Iolaos are
all written on the vase in the Corinthian
alphabet.

BLACK-FIGURED KYLIX

Attributed to the
Boread Painter
Greek (Sparta),
570 – 565 B.C.
Terracotta
H: 12 cm (4¹¹⁄₁₆ in.);
DIAM: 14 cm (5½ in.)
85.AE.121

In the relatively brief period during which vase painting
flourished in Sparta, the Boread Painter emerged as
one of the more innovative and accomplished Lakonian
craftsmen. Although creating balanced compositions
presented a challenge for ancient vase painters, here
the Boread Painter grouped his figures in a triangular
arrangement, successfully filling the circular frame
in the interior of the cup. The Corinthian hero Bellero-
phon attacks the mythical Chimaera, a fire-breathing
lion with a goat's head on its back and a snake as its tail.
As the hero thrusts his spear into the belly of the monster with his right hand, he restrains his winged steed,
Pegasos, with his left.

BLACK-FIGURED
NECK-AMPHORA

Attributed to the
Inscription Painter
Greek, "Chalcidian" (Rhegion,
South Italy), circa 540 B.C.
Terracotta
H: 39.6 cm (15⅝ in.);
DIAM: 24.9 cm (9¹³⁄₁₆ in.)
96.AE.1

A scene from Homer's *Iliad* decorates
this storage vessel. During the Trojan
War, King Rhesos of Thrace and twelve
of his men came to assist the Trojans.
Arriving too late at night to enter Troy,
the exhausted Thracians camped in
the fields outside the city, hanging their
elaborate armor in the surrounding
shrubbery. As they slept, the Greek
heroes Odysseus and Diomedes killed
them in order to steal their immortal
horses. On one side of the vase, Diomedes is about to slay Rhesos, while
on the opposite side, Odysseus murders
another Thracian. Named for the
Euboean dialect used in the inscriptions,
"Chalcidian" pottery was probably
made in Rhegion in southern Italy,
a colony of the Greek city of Chalcis.

BLACK-FIGURED
HYDRIA

Attributed to the
Eagle Painter
Caeretan (Etruria),
circa 525 B.C.
Terracotta
H: 44.6 cm (17⅞ in.);
DIAM: 33.4 cm (13 in.)
83.AE.346

The Labors of Herakles were popular
as subjects in sixth-century-B.C.
vase painting. However, although the
Museum has two examples (see the
aryballos on p. 44), the slaying of the
many-headed Hydra of Lerna was
not a very common representation. To
kill the vicious sea monster the hero
had to cut off each head and cauterize
the neck so that new heads could not
grow back. Here Herakles' nephew
Iolaos assists him. This vase was likely
made in Italy by an artist who learned
his craft in Ionia. He had as much
interest in the ornamental motifs as in
the human subjects.

White-Ground Lekythos

Attributed to Douris
(as painter)
Greek (Athens),
circa 500 B.C.
Terracotta
H: 33.5 cm (13⅛ in.);
DIAM: 12.6 cm (4⅚ in.)
84.AE.770

In a calm, evenly disposed composition around the body of the vase, two young Athenian aristocrats arm themselves in the presence of a boy and a woman. Dressed in a short chiton, one of the youths puts on his greaves, while the other holds his helmet and shield. In the field between the figures is a *kalos* inscription praising the beauty of two youths, Nikodromos and Panaitios.

Red-Figured Kylix

Attributed to the
Brygos Painter
Greek (Athens),
490 – 480 B.C.
Terracotta
H: 11.2 cm (4⅛ in.);
DIAM: 31.4 cm (12¼ in.)
85.AE.19, 86.AE.286,
and 89.AE.58

Ajax, the greatest of the Greek heroes at Troy after Achilles, rescued the latter's body from the midst of battle. Angered and humiliated at losing Achilles' armor to Odysseus by vote of their comrades (depicted on one side of the exterior), Ajax decided on revenge but then took his own life instead. Here the painter has depicted the tragic results, as Tekmessa shrouds the body of Ajax, her lover, who lies fallen on his weapon.

RED-FIGURED KYLIX

Attributed to
the Carpenter Painter
Greek (Athens),
510–500 B.C.
Terracotta
H: 11 cm (4⁵⁄₁₆ in.);
W (with handles): 38.1 cm
(15 in.); DIAM: 30.5 cm (12 in.)
85.AE.25

Athletic training was an important part of a young
Athenian's education. The scenes painted on the outside
of this cup show athletes training in the *palaestra*, or
stadium. On this side, two discus-throwers practice
their form while two jumpers (carrying weights) wait
for the youth with the hoe to prepare the track. A flutist
sways gracefully among them, melodically accompanying their exercises.

RED-FIGURED KYLIX

Attributed to Onesimos
(as painter)
Greek (Athens),
500–490 B.C.
Terracotta
H (restored): 8.3 cm (3¼ in.);
DIAM: 23.5 cm (9¼ in.);
W (with handles,
one restored):
30.5 cm (12 in.)
86.AE.607

The antics of satyrs, the part-horse, part-human companions to Dionysos, were a popular subject for the
drinking cups of Athenians. In the interior, or tondo,
of this kylix, a satyr creeps up on a nymph who naps
on a large striped cushion beneath a rocky outcropping.
The Greek inscription above them tells why the satyr
is so smitten: "The girl is beautiful." Onesimos takes
particular delight in juxtaposing the lovely profile
of the sleeping girl with the brutish pug-nosed face of
the satyr attempting to steal a kiss.

RED-FIGURED KYLIX

Signed by Douris
(as painter); attributed
to Python (as potter)
Greek (Athens), circa 480 B.C.
Terracotta
H: 13.3 cm (5³⁄₁₆ in.);
DIAM: 32.4 cm (12⅝ in.)
84.AE.569

In the interior tondo a stately bearded figure, perhaps
Kekrops, a legendary king of Athens, sits before an
altar holding a kylix that a youthful attendant fills with
wine from an *oinochoe*, or pitcher. On one side of the
exterior, the goddess Eos pursues Kephalos as Kekrops
and Pandion (both identified by inscription), another
mythological king of Athens, and a third king, perhaps
Erechtheus, look on. On the other side Zeus seizes the
Trojan prince Ganymede.

RED-FIGURED KANTHAROS WITH MASKS

Attributed to the Foundry
Painter (as painter) and to
Euphronios (as potter)
Greek (Athens), circa 480 B.C.
Terracotta
H (handles): 21.1 cm (8¼ in.);
DIAM (bowl): 17.4 cm (6¹³⁄₁₆ in.)
85.AE.263, 88.AE.150, and
96.AE.335.4–.5, .9

Restored from a number of fragments,
this cup has two fully modeled masks
attached on either side. One is the
face of Dionysos, the god of wine, the
other, the face of a satyr. Both are
appropriate decorations for a cup used
for wine. The bowl is decorated with
painted figures of youthful athletes,
each standing on a short meander band.

RED-FIGURED DINOS

Attributed to the
Syleus Painter
Greek (Athens), circa 470 B.C.
Terracotta
H: 36.8 cm (14⅛ cm);
DIAM: 35.7 cm (14 in.)
89.AE.73

Most of the names of the figures depicted
on this vessel used for mixing wine and
water are identified by inscriptions. On
the front, the beautifully rendered figure
of Triptolemos is ready to depart in his
fabulous winged chariot to spread the
knowledge of grain cultivation across
the world. Behind him, Demeter, the
goddess of vegetation and fertility, holds
stalks of grain. Facing Triptolemos is
Kore, the daughter of Demeter, who
offers a departure libation. Additional
figures encircle the vase, including
Hades, god of the Underworld; his
wife Thea; Eleusis, a personification of
the city; Hippothoon and Kalamites,
eponymous heroes of Eleusis; and an
unidentified man.

RED-FIGURED CALYX-KRATER

Signed by Syriskos
(otherwise known as the
Copenhagen painter)
Greek (Athens), 470–460 B.C.
Terracotta
H: 43 cm (16¼ in.);
DIAM: 54 cm (21¼₆ in.)
92.AE.6

Both sides of this deep vessel, which was
used for mixing wine and water, depict
unusual mythological scenes. The names
of all the figures are written beside them.
On the front, the goddess Ge Pantaleia
(all-giving Earth) sits on a throne between her son, Okeanos (Ocean), on the
left, and the god of wine, Dionysos, on
the right. Barely visible over the handle
behind Dionysos is the signature of
Syriskos. This name means "the little
Syrian," suggesting that he was a for-
eigner working in Athens.
     A unique scene is depicted on the
back side of the krater. Themis, the
Greek goddess of justice, is flanked by
Balos (Belos), the son of Poseidon
and Libya, and his maternal grandfather
Ephaphos, the son of Zeus and Io.
The price of the vase, one Greek stater,
is written under its foot. This amount
approximates two day's wages for an
Athenian soldier.

PANATHENAIC PRIZE AMPHORA AND LID

Attributed to the Painter
of the Wedding Procession
(as painter); signed by
Nikodemos (as potter)
Greek (Athens), 363 – 362 B.C.
Terracotta
H (with lid): 89.5 cm (35 in.)
93.AE.55

Panathenaic vases were given as prizes for athletic contests held every four years during the Panathenaic festi-
val in Athens. Athena, the patron goddess of Athens,
was always placed on the front, and the event commem-
orated by the vase on the back. The date of this vase
was determined by the two bordering figures of Nike,
the goddess of victory, standing atop akanthos columns,
which are unique to the years 363/362 B.C. The letters
alongside the column behind Athena spell Nikodemos,
while those along the column in front of her identify
the vase as an award.

The reverses of panathenaic amphorae were decorated with images of the contest for which the vase was
awarded. Nike prepares to crown the victorious youth,
a boxer, who has a very long ribbon of leather in his
left hand. When wrapped around the athlete's hand and
wrist, this was his boxing glove. On the left stands his
defeated opponent folding a leather thong in his hands.
The bearded man on the right is the judge of the event.

RED-FIGURED DINOID VOLUTE-KRATER AND STAND

Attributed to the
Meleager Painter
Greek (Athens), 390–380 B.C.
Terracotta
H: 70.6 cm (27½ in.);
DIAM (krater): 40.6 cm (15¹³⁄₁₆ in.)
87.AE.93

The ribbed black body of this elaborately decorated vase intentionally imitates metal vessels. The krater is ornamented with heads of Ethiopians at the handles' bases, gilded female heads in the handles' volutes, and floral and figural decoration on the neck and base. On the front of the neck is a scene featuring Adonis lying on a couch between his rival lovers, Aphrodite and Persephone. Echoing the scene on the neck, the stand shows a reclining Dionysos attended by Eros and accompanied by satyrs, maenads, and the gods Hephaistos and Apollo. Scenes of mythical and real combat decorate the shoulder of the stand, which was cut down in antiquity and has been restored on the basis of ancient parallels.

Panathenaic Prize Amphora and Lid

Attributed to the
Marsyas Painter
Greek (Athens), 340 – 339 B.C.
Terracotta
H (with lid): 99.5 cm
(38¹³⁄₁₆ in.)
79.AE.147

Over the course of their long production, Panathenaic vases were always
made in the same shape and were always
painted using the same black-figure
technique. The vase, elaborate though
it is, held the true prize: oil pressed from
olives grown in Athena's sacred groves.
This vase, like the other prize amphora
(p. 51), was awarded to a victor in the
Panathenaic games. Athletic competitions were an important part of the
city's most prestigious celebrations in
honor of their divine patroness, Athena,
who strides in typical form, spear up-
held, on the front. On the back a driver
and an armored man (*apobates*) steer
a four-horse chariot team, or *quadriga*.
In this sport, the *apobates* jumped
on and off the chariot as it raced against
the other teams.

Red-Figured Pelike of Kerch Style

Attributed to the Painter
of the Wedding Procession
Greek (Athens),
330 – 320 B.C.
Terracotta
H: 48.3 cm (18⅞ in.);
DIAM (body): 27.2 cm
(10¹¹⁄₁₆ in.)
83.AE.10

Vases in the Kerch style take their name from an area
on the Black Sea where numerous examples have been
found. The style is characterized by an elaborate and
often flamboyant use of polychromy, gilding, and relief
work to augment the simple red-on-black scheme of
earlier Attic vases. The scene represented on the front
of the vase is the Judgment of Paris, the young prince
of Troy who had to choose the most beautiful of
three goddesses: Hera, Athena, or Aphrodite. Paris sits
surrounded by the three deities with the messenger
god, Hermes, at the far left. The unrelated scene on the
back depicts two amazons fighting a Greek warrior.

RED-FIGURED BELL-KRATER

Name vase of the
Choregos Painter
Greek (Apulia, South Italy),
circa 380 B.C.
Terracotta
H: 37 cm (14⁷⁄₁₆ in.);
DIAM (mouth): 45 cm (17¾ in.)
96.AE.29

An unidentified theatrical scene is represented on the front of this vessel, which
was used to mix wine and water. The
name of each of the four players is inscribed above his head, beginning from
the left: Aigisthos, Choregos (a financial
backer), Pyrrhias, and another Choregos. Because the figures are costumed
and stand on an actual stage they appear
to be performing parts in a play, possibly a comic version of the preparations
for a stage production. One theory is
that Aigisthos, who wears tragic dress,
stands for Tragedy. Pyrrhias then represents Comedy, in the characteristic
pose of a declaimer. The remaining two
actors in masks and padded comic dress
argue over which one they will ultimately back. The reverse side shows a
genre scene: a woman sits attended by
a servant who fans her as she receives a
young male visitor.

RED-FIGURED CALYX-KRATER

Signed by Asteas (as painter)
Greek (Paestum, South Italy),
circa 340 B.C.
Terracotta
H: 71.2 cm (27¾ in.);
DIAM: 59.6 cm (23¼ in.)
81.AE.78

This impressive krater is the largest
of eleven known vases signed by Asteas,
one of only two artists from the city
of Paestum who signed his works.
Standing on an elaborately modeled
and decorated foot, the vase carries the
only Paestan representation of one of
the most popular myths in antiquity: the
love of Zeus for the mortal girl Europa.
Framed in a unique pentagonal panel,
the white bull into which Zeus transformed himself carries Europa across
the sea. Pothos, the personification of
passionate longing, flies overhead.
Various gods, including Aphrodite and
Eros, watch the scene from the upper
corners like an audience. The theatrical
aspect of the composition follows a
Sicilian tradition. On the back is depicted
a procession of the god of wine, Dionysos, and his retinue.

RED-FIGURED LOUTROPHOROS

Attributed to the Painter of
Louvre MNB 1148
Greek (Apulia, South Italy),
late fourth century B.C.
Terracotta
H: 90 cm (35⅛ in.);
DIAM (mouth): 26 cm (10⅛ in.)
86.AE.680

In one of his guises adopted while seducing mortals, Zeus appears here as a white swan leaping into Leda's embrace, while Hypnos, a personification of sleep, showers them with drowsiness. To the right and left are Leda's companions. In the Ionic building above are Zeus and Aphrodite with Eros on her arm. Zeus may be asking for Aphrodite's help in seducing Leda and using Eros to plead his case. The division of the decoration into two levels may be inspired by theatrical performances, which in antiquity often took place on different stories of the stage building. Other mythological figures—Astrape, a personification of lightning; Eniautos, the personification of the calendar year; and Eleusis, a personification of an important sanctuary—are not clearly connected to the story.

SKYPHOS AND FLASK

Roman, 25 B.C.–A.D. 25
Cameo glass (white on blue)
Skyphos H: 10.5 cm (4⅛ in.);
Flask H: 7.6 cm (3 in.)
84.AF.85, 85.AF.84

Cameo glass vessels exhibit the great skill of the artisans responsible for their manufacture and carved decoration. The skyphos is decorated with Dionysiac imagery: satyrs flanked by female figures. Its foot is a modern reconstruction. The imagery on the flask includes Erotes, a striding pharaoh, an obelisk, and an altar surmounted by the Egyptian god Thoth.

WREATH

Greek, late fourth
century B.C.
Gold, with blue and green
glass-paste inlays and glass
beads
DIAM: 30 cm (11 $^{11}/_{16}$ in.)
93.AM.30

An abundance of stemmed flowers is attached to a
circlet fashioned as two twigs that hinge at the front by
means of a "Herakles," or square, knot. The myrtle
flowers, many comprised of numerous minuscule com-
ponents, are fashioned out of thin sheet gold. Some of
the delicate petals are inlaid with blue and green glass
paste and some of the flowers have small blue glass
beads attached to the tips of their stamens, adding striking color accents to an already dazzling display of gold.
Most of the known surviving wreaths are much simpler
in design. Such elaborate wreaths may have actually
been worn in ceremonies, as they often show evidence
of repair. Customarily, they were buried with the dead
along with other precious offerings.

Ring Stone with a Portrait of Demosthenes

Signed by Apelles
Roman, first century B.C.
Carnelian and gold
Gem: 1.9 × 1.5 cm (¾ × ⅝ in.)
90.AN.13

This gem is engraved with a portrait of Demosthenes (384–322 B.C.), the city of Athens' most famous orator. It is signed *Apellou* (of Apelles) below his neck. The placement of the name surely indicates that it is the signature of the artist, and the style and motif, along with the shape of the gem and ring, suggest a date of the late first century B.C., a time when fine, signed works were in vogue.

Two-Handled Cup

Roman, first century A.D.
Silver
H: 12.5 cm (4⅞ in.);
DIAM: 16.3 cm (6⁷⁄₁₆ in.)
96.AM.57

Encircling this drinking cup is a scene that may be derived from Homer's *Odyssey*. Odysseus was instructed by the sorceress Circe to travel to the Underworld to consult the ghost of the blind seer Teiresias, the only one who could tell the hero when he would return home. Here Odysseus holds aloft his sword and averts his eyes, having slain a ram to summon the ghost. Teiresias sits in the center on a rocky outcrop, gazing sightlessly upward. On the other side five male figures (probably philosophers) converse.

Ensemble of Jewelry

Greek (possibly Alexandria),
Hellenistic, 220 – 100 B.C.
Gold with various inlaid and attached stones, including garnet, carnelian, pearl, and glass paste
92.AM.8.1 – .9

This spectacular collection of gold jewelry was surely the prized possession of a Greek woman of high social rank. The style of the pieces and the techniques used indicate that they were probably made in Alexandria, Egypt, by Greek goldsmiths during the reign of the Ptolemies, the rulers of Egypt descended from Ptolemy I Soter, one of the Macedonian generals of Alexander the Great. Signs of ancient repair show that the jewelry was not made specifically for the tomb as funerary offerings, but actually worn. Included are a hair net, a diadem, armlets, bracelets, earrings, and rings.

Plate Showing a Philosophical Debate between Ptolemy and Hermes Trismegistos

Byzantine, Late Antique,
sixth century A.D.
Silver
45 × 28 cm (17⅞ × 10⅞ in.)
83.AM.342

An unidentified man is enthroned at the top of this plate. Below, a bearded man, designated by a Greek inscription as Ptolemaeus, is seated on the left; behind him stands a woman designated as Skepsis. Facing them is a man named as Hermes, but the inscription relating to the woman with him is lost. The subject seems to be allegorical, perhaps of the philosophical dispute between Science and Mythology. If this is the case, Ptolemy, the founder of the Alexandrian school of scientific thought, is seen here in debate with Hermes Trismegistos, the exponent of traditional human wisdom as embodied in myth.

RHYTON

Eastern Greek (Seleucid
Empire), late Hellenistic,
late first century B.C.
or early first century A.D.
Gilt silver with glass-paste
and stone inlays
H: 26.5 cm (10⅜ in.);
DIAM (rim): 12.7 cm (4¹⁵⁄₁₆ in.)
86.AM.753

This gilt-silver rhyton is one of the most elaborately
decorated drinking horns to survive from antiquity.
Relief floral patterns cover the entire surface of the
curving horn, which terminates in the forequarters of
an antlered stag. Executed with exceptional attention
to anatomical detail—particularly apparent in the
veins running down the creature's face—the stag is
shown in flight. The preserved inlaid eyes of glass
paste, with the whites clearly visible, heighten the expression of fear and alertness conveyed by the stag's
raised head. Though the vessel surely was produced in
a workshop on the eastern fringes of the Hellenistic
world, the closest parallels for the ornamental designs
are found among the late Hellenistic decorative arts
created under the Seleucid rulers who inherited the
eastern part of Alexander the Great's sprawling empire.

Preserved on the belly of the animal is an inscription
in Aramaic letters that dedicates this rhyton to the
goddess Artemis.

MUMMY PORTRAIT
OF A WOMAN

Attributed to the
Isidora Master
Romano-Egyptian (Fayum),
A.D. 100 – 125
Encaustic and gilt on a
wooden panel wrapped
in linen
Panel: 33.6 × 17.2 cm
(13⅛ × 6¾ in.)
81.AP.42

Painted portraits such as this one were
usually executed from life on a square
wooden panel, then reshaped after the
subject's death and incorporated into the
linen wrappings of his or her mummy.

The liveliness, directness, and individuality of the representation support
the hypothesis that this lady sat for her
portrait sometime before her death. Her
hairstyle and jewelry help to date the
painting to the early second century A.D.

The near-perfect condition of this
panel is the result of burial conditions.

Manuscripts

At the J. Paul Getty Museum the art of the Middle Ages is represented primarily by illuminated manuscripts, books written and decorated entirely by hand. In 1983 the trustees of the Museum began the collection with the purchase of the holdings of Dr. Peter and Irene Ludwig of Aachen, Germany. The Ludwig manuscripts represent the history of the art of book illumination from the ninth to the sixteenth century. In order to provide as complete and balanced a representation as possible, about sixty-five further acquisitions have been made since 1984, including codices and cuttings or groups of leaves from individual books.

Over the course of the Middle Ages manuscripts became the most important means of recording not only scripture and liturgy but also history, literature, law, philosophy, and science, both ancient and medieval. Certain books, mainly religious service books in the early period, came to be decorated with elaborate initials, framed paintings (called miniatures), and other embellishments.

The collection includes masterpieces of Ottonian, Byzantine, Romanesque, Gothic, International style, and Renaissance illumination found in manuscripts made in Germany, France, Belgium, Italy, England, Spain, Poland, and the eastern Mediterranean. Among the highlights from the early and high Middle Ages are two Ottonian sacramentaries (see pp. 62–63); the Stammheim Missal (see pp. 66–67) and a Gospel book from Helmarshausen (see p. 64), both German Romanesque manuscripts; a French Gothic psalter (see p. 68); and an English Gothic Apocalypse (see p. 71). The holdings of late medieval French manuscripts include illuminations by the Boucicaut Master (see p. 78) and Jean Fouquet (p. 81), among others. The collection features a trove of late Flemish manuscripts, including *The Visions of the Knight Tondal*, attributed to Simon Marmion and commissioned by Margaret of York, Duchess of Burgundy (see p. 85), the Prayer Book of Cardinal Albrecht of Brandenburg with miniatures by Simon Bening (see p. 88), and the *Model Book of Calligraphy*, illuminated by Joris Hoefnagel for Emperor Rudolf II (see p. 89).

The manuscripts are exhibited on a rotating basis year-round.

SACRAMENTARY

French (Fleury),
1000–1025
Parchment, ten leaves
23.2 × 17.8 cm (9⅛ × 7⅟₁₆ in.)
Ms. Ludwig V 1;
83.MF.76
Illustration: Attributed
to Nivardus of Milan,
Decorated Initial *D*
(fol. 9)

Sacramentaries, the most important type of liturgical book used in the early medieval Church, contain the prayers said by a priest at Mass. The initial letters of the main prayers in this fragment, such as the *D* shown here, are filled with elaborate interlace ornament and foliate sprays that hark back to ninth-century Carolingian models based on late antique motifs. The lavish use of gold, silver, and purple in the decoration, which also includes a full-page *Crucifixion*, suggests that the book was made for a member of the royal circle, possibly by Nivardus of Milan, an artist known to have worked in France.

Sacramentary

German (Mainz or Fulda),
1025–1050
Parchment, 179 leaves
26.6 × 19.1 cm
(10½ × 7⁷⁄₁₆ in.)
Ms. Ludwig V 2; 83.MF.77
Illustration: *The Women at the Tomb* (fol. 19v) and cover

The seven full-page miniatures in this book of prayers to be said at Mass reveal the monumentality of Ottonian painting. Set against colored bands, these scenes from sacred history are infused with an otherworldly, timeless quality. The manuscript's luxurious binding in silver and copper gilt, showing Christ in Majesty in high relief, dates from the twelfth century.

GOSPEL BOOK

German (Helmarshausen),
circa 1120–40
Parchment, 168 leaves
22.8 × 16.4 cm (9 × 6½ in.)
Ms. Ludwig II 3; 83.MB.67
Illustration: *Saint Matthew*
(fol. 9v)

The portraits of the evangelists (Matthew, Mark, Luke,
and John) in this manuscript exemplify the Romanesque
style developed at Helmarshausen abbey, an important artistic center in northern Germany that enjoyed
the patronage of Henry the Lion, Duke of Saxony
and Bavaria (reigned 1139–1180). The compositions
are constructed from lively patterns, and the colors are
warm and saturated. The arrangement of the drapery
folds, the facial features, and the use of firm black outlines to separate areas of different colors have much
in common with the work of Roger of Helmarshausen,
a famous metalsmith active at the abbey in the early
twelfth century. Saint Matthew is shown here writing
his Gospel.

New Testament

Byzantine
(Constantinople), 1133
Parchment, 279 leaves
22 × 18 cm (8¹¹⁄₁₆ × 7⅛ in.)
Ms. Ludwig II 4; 83.MB.68
Illustration: *Saint John the
Evangelist* (fol. 106v)

The portraits of the evangelists in this New Testament
are among the finest achievements of Byzantine
illumination of the Comnenian period (named for the
Comneni emperors, who ruled from 1018 until 1185).
The artist's use of line and surface pattern to create
expressive effects is typical of the pictorial style of the
mid-twelfth century and is also to be found in monumental art.

BREVIARY

Italian (Montecassino),
1153
Parchment, 428 leaves
19.1 × 13.2 cm (7⁹⁄₁₆ × 5�³⁄₁₆ in.)
Ms. Ludwig IX 1; 83.ML.97
Illustration: Decorated
Initial *C* (fol. 138v)

Sigenulfus, the scribe of this breviary, identified himself in a prayer he penned on one of its leaves. He was a member of the monastic community at Montecassino, the cradle of the Benedictine order, which was founded in the sixth century by Saint Benedict. During the eleventh and twelfth centuries the monastery's scriptorium developed a distinctive style of decorative initial in which the paneled framework of the letter brims over with a frenzied mixture of interlaced tendrils and fantastic creatures.

STAMMHEIM MISSAL

German (Hildesheim),
circa 1160
Parchment, 184 leaves
28.2 × 18.8 cm (11⅛ × 7⁷⁄₁₆ in.)
Ms. 64; 97.MG.21
Illustration: *Saint Bernward*
(fol. 156)

The beauty of this missal's pages is matched by the theological complexity of the illumination. The miniatures and the initials—many of which include a great number of figures and inscriptions—are full of variety. The manuscript was made at and for the Benedictine monastery of Saint Michael at Hildesheim shortly after the monks had been given permission to venerate their founder, Bernward of Hildesheim, as a saint. The anonymous illuminator depicts Bishop Bernward within the monastery church. Heinrich of Midel, a contemporary monk, kneels and prays at the saint's feet.

PSALTER

French (probably Noyon),
after 1205
Parchment, 176 leaves
31 × 21.9 cm (12 ³⁄₁₆ × 8 ⅝ in.)
Ms. 66; 99.MK.48
Illustration: Master of the
Ingeborg Psalter, Initial *D*
with *David in Prayer* (fol. 108)

The style of the large painted initials in this psalter—
a book containing the psalms and other devotional
texts—represents a turning point in the history of
European art, when illuminators left behind abstract
and highly stylized painting in favor of the naturalistic
representation of the visible world. In this initial,
King David kneels in prayer as he is buffeted by a
wind—a metaphor for his afflictions. The anonymous
illuminator portrays the wind's effect not only on
David's garments but also on his hair, making the wind
as much a subject of the initial as David himself.
This attention to detail informs the naturalism of the
emerging Gothic style in painting.

Gospel Book

Byzantine (Nicaea or
Nicomedia), early and
late thirteenth century
Parchment, 241 leaves
20.5 × 15 cm (8⅛ × 5⅞ in.)
Ms. Ludwig II 5; 83.MB.69
Illustration: *The Agony in
the Garden* (fol. 68)

The extensive decoration in this Gospel book was
executed at different stages over the course of the
thirteenth century and is thus an important witness to
changes in Byzantine art at a pivotal moment in
European history. This miniature from the end of the
century is representative of the Palaeologan phase
of Byzantine art, which flourished after the Western
Crusaders were expelled from Constantinople in 1261.
The Palaeologan style (which lasted into the fifteenth
century and is named after the imperial family of the
Palaiologoi) is noted for the use of large-scale figures
based on classical models and portrayed with dramatic
gestures and intensity of feeling. With the expansive
composition of the apostles against the mountain,
the three-dimensionality evident in the drapery folds,
and the care taken to individualize each figure, *The
Agony in the Garden* stands as an impressive monument
of later Byzantine art.

PSALTER

German (Würzburg),
circa 1240–50
Parchment, 192 leaves
22.6 × 15.7 cm (8¹³⁄₁₆ × 6³⁄₁₆ in.)
Ms. Ludwig VIII 2; 83.MK.93
Illustration: *Pentecost*
(fol. 111v)

Richly illuminated psalters enjoyed widespread popularity in the thirteenth century as a form of deluxe private devotional book. The abundant decoration of this psalter includes twelve illuminated calendar pages, each decorated with the full-length figure of a prophet; six full-page miniatures depicting imagery from the Old and New Testaments; and ten elaborate, large historiated initials.

The finely chiseled features of the figures and the angular folds of their draperies are typical of thirteenth-century German illumination as practiced in Thuringia and Saxony, in the north, and in Würzburg, in the southwest, which was influenced by the northern schools. The forms of this so-called Zigzag style are remarkably expressive.

DYSON PERRINS APOCALYPSE

English (probably London),
circa 1255–60
Parchment, forty-one leaves
31.9 × 22.5 cm (12⅝ × 8⅞ in.)
Ms. Ludwig III 1; 83.MC.72
Illustration: *The Opening
of the First Seal: The First
Horseman* (fol. 6)

A fashion for richly illustrated copies of the Apocalypse, Saint John's vision of the end of the world as recorded in the New Testament Book of Revelation, developed in England in the mid-thirteenth century. In manuscripts such as this one, which contains eighty-two half-page miniatures, aristocratic lay patrons could contemplate the calamitous events Saint John described through pictures as well as text.

Remarkable for their lively interpretation of the saint's vision, the miniatures show him witnessing the extraordinary events as they occur. The figures were outlined in pen and ink and then modeled with thin, colored washes. Their elegant poses, the graceful contours of the forms, and the decorative patterns of the drapery folds typify early English Gothic illumination at its finest.

Canon Tables from the Zeytʿun Gospels

Armenian (Hromklay), 1256
Parchment, eight leaves
26.5 × 19 cm (10⁷/₁₆ × 7½ in.)
Ms. 59; 94.MB.71
Illustration: Tʿoros Roslin,
canons 7 and 8 (fol. 6)

Canon tables present a concordance of passages relating the same events in the four Gospels. Canon table pages were an important field for decoration in manuscript Bibles and Gospel books throughout the Middle Ages, the columns of numbers inviting an architectural treatment. On this page, the Armenian illuminator Tʿoros Roslin has placed the text within a grand and brilliantly colored architecture that includes animal heads and human faces, and he has enlivened the page with a variety of plants and birds.

ANTIPHONAL

Italian (Bologna), late
thirteenth century
Parchment, 243 leaves
58.2 × 40.2 cm
(22 15/16 × 15 13/16 in.)
Ms. Ludwig VI 6; 83.MH.89
Illustration: Master of
Gerona, Initial *A* with
Christ in Majesty (fol. 2)

This manuscript is the first volume of a multivolume
antiphonal, a compilation of chants for the Divine
Office, the services celebrated at regular intervals
throughout the day. Like all liturgical choir books, its
format is large so that all members of the choir could
see the music it contains. It may have been made for the
monastery of San Jacopo de Ripoli, outside Florence,
since the same artist provided that religious community
with at least two other choir books. He probably trained
in Bologna, a major center of Gothic art in Italy. The
facial types, abstract patterns of drapery highlights, and
certain iconographic motifs in this antiphonal reflect
the impact of Byzantine art. The brilliant luminosity
and monumental figure style achieved by the artist link
his work with the most important Bolognese manuscripts produced at this time.

The following text appears within the illuminated page:

digandar por render uithcia
o non render o por fazer conf
tíe'ìnimímíéros o por non fa
zer por fazer complir laf fen
reneìas. o quoalcs & qmere
onas aceones por razon de v

fa nun reeba o
palauras o por
nos. &caf acad
oiros fin toro p
garim. fin con
enro. riendta a

VIDAL MAYOR

Spanish (northeastern Spain),
circa 1290–1310
Parchment, 277 leaves
36.5 × 24 cm (14⅜ × 9⁷⁄₁₆ in.)
Ms. Ludwig XIV 6; 83.MQ.165
Illustration: Initial *N* with
*King James I of Aragon
Overseeing a Court of Law*
(fol. 72v)

This sumptuous volume is the only known copy of the
law code of Aragon, which King James I (reigned 1214–
1276) ordered Vidal de Canellas, the Bishop of Huesca,
to compile in 1247. The manuscript, a translation into
the vernacular (Navarro-Aragonese), probably was
made for one of James's royal successors. It is illustrated
with ten large and numerous small scenes set into
initials. The style of illumination, painted in primary
colors, emulates Parisian court art in both the settings
and the slender figural and facial types.

VITA BEATAE HEDWIGIS

Silesian, 1353
Parchment, 204 leaves
34.1 × 24.8 cm (13⁷/₁₆ × 9¾ in.)
Ms. Ludwig XI 7; 83.MN.126
Illustration: *Saint Hedwig of Silesia with Duke Ludwig of Liegnitz and Brieg and Duchess Agnes* (fol. 12v)

This manuscript is the earliest illustrated *Life of the Blessed Hedwig*, whose subject was a thirteenth-century duchess of Silesia (a duchy on the border between Poland and Germany). It contains one of the masterpieces of Central European manuscript illumination: a full-page miniature of Saint Hedwig herself. Hedwig, who founded a number of religious houses in Silesia, carries a book, prayer beads, and a small statue of the Virgin, all references to her devout character. The small-scale donor portraits represent Duke Ludwig I of Liegnitz and Brieg, the saint's descendant, and his wife, Agnes, who commissioned the manuscript in 1353.

Two Miniatures

German (Cologne),
circa 1400–10
Parchment
23.6 × 12.5 cm (9⁵⁄₁₆ × 4⁷⁄₈ in.)
Ms. Ludwig Folia 2; 83.MS.49
Illustration: Master of Saint
Veronica, *The Crucifixion*
(leaf 1)

The courtly elegance of the International style is captured in the rich costumes, brilliantly diapered backgrounds, and softly modeled forms of this *Crucifixion*
and its companion miniature, *Saint Anthony*. Attributed
to the Master of Saint Veronica, a leading artist of
Cologne, these leaves may once have been part of a
liturgical manuscript.

RUDOLF VON EMS, WELTCHRONIK

Bavarian (Regensburg),
circa 1400–10
Parchment, 309 leaves
33.5 × 23.5 cm (13¹⁄₁₆ × 9¼ in.)
Ms. 33; 88.MP.70
Illustration: *Moses' Vision
of the Back of God's Head;
Moses' Shining Face and the
Ark of the Covenant* (fol. 89v)

The World Chronicle of Rudolf von Ems was written in
rhymed couplets that weave biblical, classical, and other
secular texts into a continuous history of the world
beginning with Creation. This miniature depicts two
scenes: an unusual representation of Moses' vision of
the back of God's head (Exodus 33:12–23) and Moses
after his descent from Mount Sinai (Exodus 34:29–35).
He is represented with horns, the result of a medieval
misunderstanding of Saint Jerome's translation of the
original Hebrew text.

The vigorous, broadly painted miniatures with contrasting, often incandescent colors find few parallels
in European art of the first half of the fifteenth century.
The miniatures of *The World Chronicle* have a bold
narrative style; the figures have intense expressions
and interact dramatically. The identity of the original
owner, undoubtedly an important nobleman, is
unknown. Duke Albert IV of Bavaria (reigned 1463–
1508) and Duchess Kunigunde owned the manuscript
later in the fifteenth century.

GIOVANNI
BOCCACCIO, *DES*
CAS DES NOBLES
HOMMES ET FEMMES

French (Paris), circa 1415
Parchment, 318 leaves
42 × 29.6 cm
(16⅜ × 11¹¹⁄₁₆ in.)
Ms. 63; 96.MR.17
Illustration: Boucicaut Master
and Workshop, *Samson and
the Lion* (fol. 26v)

The Florentine poet Giovanni Boccaccio (1313–1375)
is best known today for the *Decameron*, one of the great
early works of fiction written in Italian. In the later
Middle Ages, however, *The Fates of Illustrious Men and
Women*, written in Latin, was one of his most popular
efforts. It relates the stories of notables from biblical,
classical, and medieval history. Laurent de Premierfait,
who translated the text into French, embellished the
original with many colorful tales from other authors,
including Livy (59 B.C.–A.D. 17) and Valerius Maximus
(fl. circa A.D. 20).

The first quarter of the fifteenth century proved to
be one of the most original and influential epochs of
Parisian manuscript illumination, due in significant part
to the genius and industriousness of the anonymous
illuminator called the Boucicaut Master. With the aid
of numerous highly trained collaborators, this artist's
work became known throughout Europe and influenced
not only the direction of French illumination for more
than a generation but that of Flemish painting as well.

BOOK OF HOURS

French (probably Paris),
circa 1415–25
Parchment, 247 leaves
20.1 × 15 cm (7¹⁵/₁₆ × 5⅞ in.)
Ms. 57; 94.ML.26
Illustration: Spitz Master, *The Flight into Egypt* (fol. 103v)

The primary artist of this book of hours was deeply versed in the art of the International style, especially that of the Limbourg Brothers (circa 1386–1416), the official painters of one of the great patrons of manuscripts, John, Duke of Berry. Indeed, seven miniatures in this book draw upon compositions of the Limbourgs from the duke's *Très Riches Heures* (Chantilly, Musée Condé) and *Belles Heures* (New York, The Cloisters). The Spitz Master, however, departs from the elegant, sophisticated style of the Limbourgs; his art is both more playful and more direct. In this miniature, for example, the threatening presence of Herod's soldiers, in pursuit of the Holy Family as they flee to Egypt, is communicated by their exaggerated size. The Spitz Master expanded on the narratives of a number of the miniatures by including scenes in the borders. Here the apocryphal story of the Miracle of the Wheat Field is depicted.

Book of Hours

Flemish (probably Ghent),
circa 1450–55
Parchment, 286 leaves
19.4 × 14 cm (7⅝ × 5½ in.)
Ms. 2; 84.ML.67
Illustration: Master of Guille-
bert de Mets, *Saint George
and the Dragon* (fol. 18v)

This deluxe manuscript, with gigantic, brightly colored foliage wending through its borders, exemplifies the inventive, often playful character of the decorated borders in Flemish manuscripts. The acanthus leaves dwarf Saint George and the princess, whom he has rescued from the dragon. The anonymous illuminator was a leading Flemish artist in the first half of the fifteenth century.

HOURS OF SIMON DE VARIE

French (Tours and
perhaps Paris), 1455
Parchment, ninety-seven
leaves
11.5 × 8.2 cm (4½ × 3¼ in.)
Ms. 7; 85.ML.27
Illustration: Jean Fouquet,
*Coat of Arms Held by a
Woman and a Greyhound*
(fol. 2v)

This heraldic miniature and the three other frontispiece
miniatures in this book of hours are the work of Jean
Fouquet, one of the great fifteenth-century French
painters. Influenced by Italian Renaissance painting, the
figural style and compositions in Fouquet's miniatures
have a geometric simplicity and monumentality that
transformed French art. His technical mastery is evident in the flesh tones of the woman, rendered in points
of color invisible to the naked eye, and in the transpar-
ent cascade of hair through which the background of
the miniature can be seen. Fouquet, a panel painter
as well as an illuminator, worked successively at the
courts of Charles VII (reigned 1422–1461) and Louis XI
(reigned 1461–1483) of France.

   This manuscript is a portion of a book of hours made
for Simon de Varie, a high official at the royal court.
De Varie's mottoes appear in the borders of the miniatures. In this one *Vie à mon Desir* (Life according to
one's desire), an anagram of his name, is inscribed on
the collar of the heraldic dog supporting the arms.
Separated from the Getty volume in the seventeenth
century, the two other portions of the book are now in
the Royal Library at The Hague.

MINIATURE

Italian (possibly Mantua),
circa 1460–70
Parchment
20.1 × 12.9 cm (7¹⁵⁄₁₆ × 5⁄₁₆ in.)
Ms. 55; 94.MS.13
Illustration: Girolamo da
Cremona, *Pentecost* (recto)

Girolamo da Cremona (active circa 1455–1483) was one
of the major interpreters of the new Renaissance style
in the art of book illumination. An itinerant artist,
he worked for patrons in Ferrara, Padua, Mantua, Siena,
and Florence, ending his career in Venice, where he
was engaged primarily in the illumination of deluxe
printed books. From 1461 to 1470 he seems to have been
at work in Mantua, having been recommended to the
Gonzaga court by Andrea Mantegna. Girolamo's debt
to Mantegna is clearly seen in this miniature, which
probably came from a book of hours or a liturgical
manuscript. The pervasive classicism, the sculptural
quality of the modeling, and the sense of symmetry and
order are all trademarks of Mantegna's style. The illusionistic frame and the expansive space of the grand
architectural setting indicate that Girolamo conceived
of this miniature as monumental in its effect.

PRAYER BOOK OF CHARLES THE BOLD

Flemish (Antwerp
and Ghent), 1469
Parchment, 159 leaves
12.4 × 9.2 cm (4⅞ × 3⅝ in.)
Ms. 37; 89.ML.35
Illustration: Attributed to the
Master of Mary of Burgundy,
The Deposition (fol. 111v)

Late medieval religious imagery sought to heighten the immediacy of the story of Christ, especially of the Passion, the events of his persecution and death. This small miniature showing the removal of Christ's body from the cross draws us close to the event's meaning by holding up for our inspection his limp and fragile corpse. It is an early work by an anonymous illuminator known as the Master of Mary of Burgundy.

Documents of payment survive for portions of this prayer book. It was commissioned by Charles the Bold, the Duke of Burgundy and son of Duke Philip the Good, the greatest of Burgundian bibliophiles. In 1469 payments were made to the scribe Nicolas Spierinc of Ghent, whose beautiful script, with its elaborate flourishes and cadelles, made him the finest of fifteenth-century Flemish scribes, and to the illuminator Lieven van Lathem of Antwerp, who was aided by several artists. The Master of Mary of Burgundy was the youngest and most gifted among them.

GUALENGHI-D'ESTE HOURS

Italian (Ferrara), circa 1469
Parchment, 211 leaves
10.8 × 7.9 cm (4¼ × 3⅛ in.)
Ms. Ludwig IX 13; 83.ML.109
Illustration: Taddeo Crivelli,
The Annunciation (fol. 3v)

This tiny, richly illuminated book of hours is one
of the finest examples of manuscript illumination from
the school of Ferrara, whose ruling family, the Este,
were ambitious bibliophiles and patrons of the arts.
The humanist values of their court and, more generally,
the Renaissance culture that flourished in much of Italy
are reflected in the classical details of the architecture,
carved stone inscriptions, and putti in the borders. Like
other painters from Ferrara, Crivelli used deep shadows
and bright highlights to model figures, giving them
their characteristic sculptural quality. The manuscript
was made for Orsina d'Este and Andrea Gualengo, who
were married in 1469.

ample ouuerte et moult
obscure. Ceste vallee estoit
tres-parfonde plaine de
charbons ardans. Et sur
icelle vallee auoit vng
couuercle de fer en ronde
tout autant moult grant
et massif a merueilles.
De celle horrible vallee par
tout tres-obscure la puan
teur qui en sentir sourmo
toit toutes les puantres
Ha. ceur que onq ame
sentist. Sur cest couuercle
descendoit lors vne grant
multitude de ames &c mp

nees qui estoient illecq
bruslees et arses et fuxt
couslees et passees parmy
cestuy audant couuercle en
la momenx que len passe
vne saulse parmy lestoam
ne. et ainsi de la cheoient
ou feu dessoubz charbons
ardans. Et la estoient les
tourmens a toute heure
renouuellez. Quant
lame de tondal apperchut
la grant horrible dieulx
tourmens elle en fut ton
tecesponuentee si ainsi entre
grant paour a lanitele

Les Visions du Chevalier Tondal

Flemish (Valenciennes
and Ghent), 1475
Parchment, forty-five leaves
36.3 × 26.2 cm
(14⁷⁄₁₆ × 10⁵⁄₁₆ in.)
Ms. 30; 87.MN.141
Illustration: Attributed to
Simon Marmion, *The Valley
of Homicides* (fol. 13v)

The Visions of the Knight Tondal is a medieval cautionary tale about a wealthy Irish knight whose soul embarks on a dreamlike journey through hell, purgatory, and heaven, during which he learns the wages of sin and the value of penitence. Written in Latin in the middle of the twelfth century, the popular story was translated into fifteen European languages over the next three centuries. This sumptuous manuscript, commissioned by Margaret of York, Duchess of Burgundy, is the only known illuminated copy of the text and contains twenty miniatures. In the scene illustrated here, Tondal's guardian angel shows the soul of the knight a burning valley in which murderers' souls are cooked on an iron lid. Above it the slim, naked figures of the damned rise and fall in a graceful ballet of torment.

MINIATURE FROM VALERIUS MAXIMUS, *FAITS ET DITS MÉMORABLES DES ROMAINS*

Flemish (Bruges),
circa 1475–80
Parchment
17.5 × 19.4 cm (6¹⁵⁄₁₆ × 7⅝ in.)
Ms. 43; 91.MS.81
Illustration: Master of the
Dresden Prayer Book,
*The Temperate and
the Intemperate* (recto)

The Memorable Deeds and Sayings of the Romans is a compilation of stories about ancient customs and heroes. Originally written in Latin in the first century by Valerius Maximus (fl. A.D. 20), it was read during much of the Middle Ages. Loosely organized by moral and philosophical categories (Temperance, Charity, Cruelty, etc.), it served as a textbook of rhetorical exercises. This cutting derives from a sumptuous large-scale copy of the French translation commissioned by Charles V of France (reigned 1364–1380), which was made for Jan Crabbe, abbot of the Cistercian abbey of Duinen, south of Bruges. The miniature shows Valerius instructing the Emperor Tiberius (to whom the text is dedicated) on the value of temperance. The upper classes and clergy shown at the back illustrate this virtue, while lower-class characters descend gleefully to illustrate its opposite. In the work of this wry illuminator from Bruges, the appropriate behavior seems staid, while the poor example amuses us.

Spinola Hours

Flemish (Ghent or
Mechelen), circa 1510–20
Parchment, 312 leaves
23.2 × 16.6 cm (9⅛ × 6⁹⁄₁₆ in.)
Ms. Ludwig IX 18; 83.ML.114
Illustration: Gerard Horen-
bout, *The Annunciation*
(fol. 92v)

In one of the most inventive page designs of sixteenth-century manuscript illumination, Gerard Horenbout has unified the traditionally separate zones of miniature and decorated border. The main subject, the Annunciation, shown taking place in the Virgin Mary's chamber, is portrayed in the middle of the page. The exterior of the building, where angels joyously pick flowers in the Virgin's garden, is depicted in the surrounding border. Thus the setting of the miniature has expanded beyond its traditional boundaries to fill the page and incorporate additional devotional stories and events.

PRAYER BOOK
OF CARDINAL
ALBRECHT
OF BRANDENBURG

Flemish (Bruges),
circa 1525–30
Parchment, 337 leaves
16.8 × 11.5 cm (6⅝ × 4½ in.)
Ms. Ludwig IX 19; 83.ML.115
Illustration: Simon Bening,
The Baptism of Christ
(fol. 58v)

Albrecht of Brandenburg's prayer book represents one
of the pinnacles in the career of the illustrious Flemish
illuminator Simon Bening. The forty-one full-page
miniatures in this book dramatically recount Christ's
childhood and ministry followed by his persecution,
Crucifixion, and Resurrection. The artist inspires the
reader's compassion and understanding through the
depiction of Christ as a vulnerable man. In the Baptism,
shown here, the spirit of God descends as a shining
dove on the frail figure of Jesus.

MIRA

CALLIGRAHIAE

MONUMENTA

Vienna, 1561–62
and circa 1591–96
Parchment, 150 leaves
16.6 × 12.4 cm (6⁹⁄₁₆ × 4⅞ in.)
Ms. 20; 86.MV.527
Illustration: Joris Hoefnagel,
Carnation and Walnut (fol. 74)

Originally written for the Holy Roman Emperor
Ferdinand I (reigned 1556–1564), the *Model Book of
Calligraphy* is a compendium of display scripts by
one of the great scribes of the Renaissance. The calligraphy on each page represents a different style
of writing inventively arranged. Thirty years later,
Emperor Rudolf II (reigned 1576–1612), Ferdinand I's
grandson, commissioned Hoefnagel to illuminate the
same pages.

Paintings

During his lifetime J. Paul Getty purchased paintings from every major European school of art between the thirteenth and twentieth centuries. He did not, however, consider himself a collector of paintings. His writings, especially his diaries, repeatedly name the decorative arts as his first love. He also felt that the best paintings were already in museums. Significant pieces of furniture, however, could still be acquired, and for much less money than a first-class painting.

Nevertheless Getty began his painting and decorative arts collections at about the same time: during the 1930s. By World War II he owned two major pictures, Gainsborough's portrait of James Christie (see p. 142) and Rembrandt's *Portrait of Marten Looten* (see p. 4), as well as a number of lesser paintings. Getty again began to collect paintings actively in the 1950s, although it was not until the middle of the following decade that he attempted to buy pictures that equaled the stature of individual pieces in his decorative arts holdings. Curiously, he never bought paintings to complement the French furniture he collected with such enthusiasm.

During the last decade of his life, Getty gave funds to the Museum that allowed it to acquire paintings from periods he had not previously found interesting. When he left the bulk of his estate to the Museum, the opportunity presented itself to acquire major works on a wider scale; these pictures, which number more than half of the paintings on exhibit, have significantly transformed the galleries.

During Getty's years as a collector, he succeeded in gathering a representative group of Italian Renaissance and Baroque paintings, plus a few Dutch figurative works of importance. In recent years these collections have been expanded. The French and Dutch schools have been much strengthened, and later French pictures by the Impressionists and their successors have been added. As a result, there is a greater overall balance of holdings from the earlier periods until the end of the nineteenth century. More significantly, the works now displayed are often more representative and important examples than in the past.

It is expected that the Museum will continue to acquire and exhibit paintings of the highest quality during the coming years, to complete the collection's transformation from a fairly small personal holding into a moderately sized but exceptionally choice public repository.

BERNARDO DADDI

Italian, circa 1280–1348
The Virgin Mary with Saints Thomas Aquinas and Paul,
circa 1330
Tempera on panel
Central panel: 120.7 × 55.9 cm
(47½ × 22 in.); left panel:
105.5 × 28 cm (41½ × 11 in.);
right panel: 105.5 × 27.6 cm
(41½ × 10⅞ in.)
93.PB.16

Reflecting the burgeoning cult of the Virgin Mary in fourteenth-century Italy, the triptych with an image of the Madonna in the central panel, flanked by standing saints in the wings, was one of the most popular forms of devotional imagery. Here, the Virgin reads the Magnificat (Luke 1:46–48) and gestures downward, perhaps referring to a tomb or an altar over which the triptych was placed. On the left, gesturing toward her, is Saint Thomas Aquinas, displaying the text of Ecclesiastes 12:9–10, one of his attributes. On the right is Saint Paul, carrying a book of his epistles and the sword by which he was martyred. These saints were probably chosen because they had some special significance to the unknown patron of the triptych.

The leading painter of his generation in Florence, Daddi was renowned for creating affecting images. Here, the Madonna is at once serene and majestic. The elegant and graceful forms of the figures, the resonant colors, and the exquisitely tooled gold all lend to the ethereal effect of this well-preserved work.

MASACCIO

(Tommaso di Giovanni Guidi)
Italian, 1401–1428
Saint Andrew, 1426
Tempera on panel
45.1 × 30.8 cm (17¾ × 12⅛ in.)
79.PB.61

This image of Saint Andrew holding his traditional symbols, a cross and book, comes from the only securely documented altarpiece by Masaccio, a polyptych painted in 1426 for the private chapel of Giuliano da San Giusto, a wealthy notary, in the church of the Carmine in Pisa. The panel was positioned on the right side of the upper tier, so that Andrew once appeared to gaze sadly toward the central panel depicting the Crucifixion.

The *Saint Andrew* exemplifies Masaccio's contribution to the founding of an early Renaissance painting style. The single figure is endowed with volume and solidity; his simplified draperies fall in sculptural folds. Since the panel stood high above the ground, the figure is slightly foreshortened for viewing from below. Furthermore, Masaccio has abandoned the elegant detachment of earlier styles in favor of a naturalistic treatment of emotion. It was this powerful combination of three-dimensional form and bold expression that so impressed his contemporaries.

GENTILE DA
FABRIANO

Italian, circa 1370–1427
The Coronation of the Virgin,
circa 1420
Tempera on panel
87.5 × 64 cm (34½ × 25½ in.)
77.PB.92

Probably painted for a church in Fabriano, Italy, Gentile's *Coronation* once formed part of a double-sided standard carried on a pole during religious processions. Stylistically it occupies the borderline between the essentially Gothic International style and the early Florentine Renaissance. Traces of the former linger in the richly patterned surfaces of the hanging and robes, which, however, clothe solidly constructed figures. The folds create a sense of volume as well as pattern, and the figures gesture with convincing naturalism.

VITTORE CARPACCIO

Italian, 1460/65–1525/26
Hunting on the Lagoon,
circa 1490–95
Oil on panel
75.4 × 63.8 cm (29¾ × 25⅛ in.)
79.PB.72

One side of this painting shows bowmen hunting birds; the other is a trompe l'oeil painting of a letter rack. The marks of hinges on the latter side indicate that this panel once functioned as a decorative shutter or cabinet door. It is a fragment of a composition that included two women on a balcony with the lagoon visible between them.

BARTOLOMMEO VIVARINI

Italian, circa 1432–1499
Polyptych with the Madonna and Child, Saint James Major, and Various Saints, 1490
Tempera on panel
280 × 215 cm (110¼ × 84⅝ in.)
71.PB.30

Shown in this altarpiece are Saints Catherine and Ursula, the Virgin and Child, and Saints Apollonia, Mary Magdalene, John the Baptist, John the Evangelist, James Major, Bartholomew, and Peter.

ANDREA MANTEGNA

Italian, circa 1431–1506
The Adoration of the Magi,
circa 1495–1505
Distemper on linen
54.6 × 69.2 cm (21½ × 27⅛ in.)
85.PA.417

Paintings of the Adoration of the Magi traditionally provided the opportunity to create grandiose scenes of Oriental richness. But for this private devotional work, Mantegna exhibited the spirit of Renaissance humanism by concentrating on the psychological interactions among the principal characters in the sacred narrative. The close-up scheme of half-length figures compressed within a shallow space and set before a neutral background was created by the artist from his study of ancient Roman reliefs, reflecting the Renaissance interest in reviving classical antiquity.

The magi, or kings, represent the three parts of the then-known world—Europe, Asia, and Africa—and personify royal recognition of Christ's superior kingship. They offer their gifts in vessels of carved agate, Turkish tombac ware, and an early example of Chinese porcelain in Europe. The subject was particularly appropriate for the painting's probable patrons, the Gonzaga family, rulers of Mantua who employed Mantegna as court painter from 1459 until his death.

Mantegna employed an unusual technique—thin washes of pigment in animal glue—resulting in dazzling color and a matte surface emphasizing the refined draftsmanship and brushwork. Although the image is somewhat darkened by varnish added at a later date (now mostly removed), the refinement of painting and the richness of detail still attest to Mantegna's mastery.

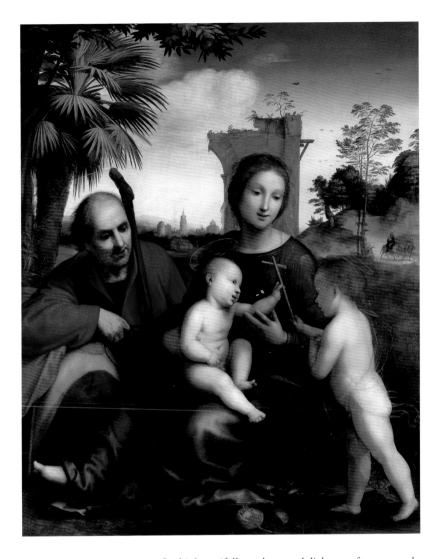

FRA BARTOLOMMEO

(Baccio della Porta)
Italian, 1472 – 1517
The Rest on the Flight into Egypt with Saint John the Baptist, circa 1509
Oil on panel
129.5 × 106.6 cm (51 × 42 in.)
96.PB.15

In this beautifully orchestrated dialogue of gesture and glance, the Holy Family, having escaped Bethlehem and King Herod's massacre of the innocents, take their ease beneath a date palm tree. Mary and Joseph look on as the infant Baptist greets the Christ Child. The unusual inclusion of John the Baptist in a Rest on the Flight can be explained by the saint's status as a patron of Florence. He is also a poignant reminder that the ultimate purpose of the Child's escape is his sacrifice on the cross. Fra Bartolommeo reinforces the pathos by depicting a pomegranate, a fruit that prefigures Christ's death, and the sheltering palm, whose fronds would pave the Savior's final entry into Jerusalem. The ruined arch alludes to the downfall of the pagan order and the rise of Christ's Church, personified by Mary.

DOSSO DOSSI

(Giovanni di Niccolò
de Lutero)
Italian, circa 1490–1542
An Allegory of Fortune,
circa 1530
Oil on canvas
178 × 216.5 cm (70½ × 85½ in.)
89.PA.32

The nude woman represents Fortune, or Lady Luck, the indifferent force that determines fate. She holds a cornucopia, flaunting the bounty that she might bring, but sits on a bubble because her favors were often fleeting. The billowing drapery serves as a reminder that she is as inconstant as the wind, and she wears only one shoe to symbolize that she is capable of bestowing not only fortune but also misfortune.

The man, a personification of Chance, looks toward Fortune as he is about to deposit lots or lottery tickets in a golden urn. This was not a traditional attribute, but a reference to the civic lotteries with cash prizes that had recently become popular in Italy. The painting was probably made for Isabella d'Este (1474–1539), Marchioness of Mantua, one of whose emblems was a bundle of lots.

The luminous, poetic coloring and atmosphere of Dosso's earlier work, adopted from Venetian paintings, here gives way to heroically proportioned and posed figures revealed by strong lighting, which the artist developed from studying Michelangelo's work in Rome.

JACOPO PONTORMO

(Jacopo Carucci)
Italian, 1494–1557
*Portrait of a Halberdier
(Francesco Guardi?)*, 1528–30
Oil or oil and tempera on
panel transferred to canvas
92 × 72 cm (36¼ × 28⅜ in.)
89.PA.49

Jacopo Pontormo was one of the founders of the so-called Mannerist style in Italy. After Michelangelo he is recognized as the most important Florentine painter of the sixteenth century. He and his pupil Bronzino excelled as portraitists, and the *Halberdier* is Pontormo's greatest achievement.

In 1568 the most famous contemporary recorder of artists' lives, the painter Giorgio Vasari, noted that Pontormo painted a most beautiful work, a portrait of Francesco Guardi, during the 1528–30 siege of Florence. We know nothing about Francesco Guardi's appearance, yet he was born in 1514, so he could be the teenage sitter.

Pontormo shows his halberdier before a bastion suggesting the defense of Florence. This youth is posed like some new Saint George or David guarding his city. His casual, swaggering pose is confident. His loose grip on the halberd (spear) and slung sword suggests a control that his expression belies. Pontormo conveys the sitter's unease with such vitality that we too feel startled as we meet his gaze.

CORREGGIO

(Antonio Allegri)
Italian, 1489/94–1534
Head of Christ, circa 1525–30
Oil on panel
26.8 × 23 cm (11¼ × 9⁹⁄₁₆ in.)
94.PB.74

Correggio, the foremost High Renaissance artist of the Emilian school, invented a type of devotional imagery in which the protagonists seem to be caught in vibrant, realistic moments. The *Head of Christ* is a mature work intended for contemplation and private prayer. The subject derives from the legend of Saint Veronica. When Christ fell on the way to the Crucifixion, he was comforted by Veronica, who wiped his face with her veil and then discovered his likeness miraculously impressed upon it. Instead of depicting the traditional iconic image of the Savior's face imprinted on the veil, Correggio portrays a hauntingly naturalistic Christ who turns toward the viewer and parts his lips as if to speak. Veronica's veil is the folded white cloth background that wraps around Christ's shoulder and ends in soft white fringes at the lower right. The painting's profound impact as a devotional image depends upon Correggio's bold invention of showing Christ wrapped within the veil the instant before the miracle. It is the living face of Christ and not his image that turns to confront the viewer.

GIULIO ROMANO

(Giulio Pippi)
Italian, before 1499–1546
The Holy Family, circa
1520–23
Oil (possibly mixed with
tempera) on panel
77.8 × 61.9 cm
(30⅝ × 24⅜ in.)
95.PB.64

Guilio Romano was Raphael's most important protégé
during his later years in Rome. This work was executed
not long after his master's death in 1520, when his own
artistic personality was beginning to come into its
own. Guilio created a cleverly orchestrated group that
is solidly classical in the tradition of Raphael, but beginning to show signs of the complicated, interlocking
compositions of the Mannerist style that he was instrumental in forging. Likewise, this painting foreshadows
other aspects of Guilio's mature style, including a
metallic palette, heavy physiognomies, and preoccupation with surface ornamentation.

Guilio sets this familiar subject at a specific time
and place. He illustrates the meeting of the Christ
Child and John the Baptist, thought to have taken place
following the Jewish ceremony of Purification, when
a new mother sacrifices turtle doves, such as those carried by the women in the background.

SEBASTIANO DEL
PIOMBO

(Sebastiano Luciani)
Italian, circa 1485–1547
Pope Clement VII,
circa 1531
Oil on slate
105.5 × 87.5 cm
(41½ × 34½ in.)
92.PC.25

This portrait depicts Giulio de' Medici (1478–1534), who reigned as Pope Clement VII from 1523 to 1534. An outstanding humanist, Clement is principally remembered as one of the greatest patrons of the Renaissance, commissioning major works from Raphael and Michelangelo as well as Sebastiano.

Michelangelo regarded Sebastiano as the greatest portrait painter of his day. The distinctive, monumental grandeur of his style was particularly suited to state portraits such as this one. The painter's characterization of the pope reflects the Renaissance cult of individuality in its bold projection of a powerful, unmistakable presence. The pontiff possesses an innate nobility and self-confidence, befitting both his position and his personality.

Aspiring to eternalize his works, Sebastiano began to experiment with painting on stone, rather than canvas or wood, in about 1530. The pope, apparently sharing the desire for an immortal image, had commissioned this portrait on slate by July 22, 1531, when the painter wrote to Michelangelo about it.

TITIAN AND WORKSHOP

(Tiziano Vecellio)
Italian, circa 1480/90–1576
Venus and Adonis,
circa 1555–60
Oil on canvas
160 × 196.5 cm (63 × 77⅜ in.)
92.PA.42

Titian won an international reputation through his portraits and mythological paintings. Most famous among the latter was a series of loves of the ancient gods—originally painted in 1554 for Philip II of Spain—that included a *Venus and Adonis*. Many of the canvases from this series were replicated and sold across Europe. The Getty *Venus and Adonis* shows Titian rethinking the Spanish original, and this version seems to have been the archetype for a cartoon that was used to generate several exact copies.

Titian depicts Venus, the goddess of love, beseeching Adonis to stay. Instead, he follows his eager hounds to his fatal encounter with a wild boar. Cupid's slumbering form and the upturned wine vase remind us that love will have no power over the lure of adventure that draws the hunter to his doom.

Venetian painters were famous for their sensuous treatment of light on textured surfaces. In *Venus and Adonis* the dog's rough fur, the glowing flesh, and the shimmering drapery glisten under the shafts of light. Forms are evoked, not described, to convey the lovers' final moment together.

FRANCESCO SALVIATI

(Francesco de' Rossi)
Italian, 1510–1563
Portrait of a Man, circa
1550–55
Oil on panel
108.9 × 86.3 cm (42⅞ × 34 in.)
86.PB.476

The bold pose, affected gesture, strident colors, and glossy finish of this likeness are characteristic of mid-sixteenth-century Mannerism. Frozen images of aristocratic rank developed from portraits such as Pontormo's *Halberdier* (see p. 99). However, this likeness reflects the influence of Pontormo's greatest pupil, Bronzino, whose portraits of the Medici court Salviati studied in the 1540s.

DOMENICHINO

(Domenico Zampieri)
Italian, 1581–1641
The Way to Calvary,
circa 1610
Oil on copper
53.7 × 68.3 cm (21⅛ × 26⅞ in.)
83.PC.373

Domenichino continually sought ideal form and grandeur, known as *disegno*, in his compositions; this painting is one of the earliest realizations of that goal. He often painted on copper plates, using small, controlled brushstrokes to describe the massive volumes of the figures. As they lean over the fallen Christ, the tormentors embody the inexorable forces driving him to Calvary. Intent on their cruelty, they do not acknowledge Christ's pleading silence.

DOMENICO FETTI

Italian, circa 1589–1623
*Portrait of a Man with a
Sheet of Music*, circa 1620
Oil on canvas
173 × 130 cm (68 × 51⅛ in.)
93.PA.17

Even though the identity of the sitter
remains a mystery, he surely represents
either a musician or an actor because
he holds a sheet of music and intensely
regards the viewer while singing or
speaking. In the background, one man
gestures for another to keep quiet,
as if the protagonist were rehearsing or
performing. Based on the overturned
cup in the lower left corner, it has been
suggested that the sitter may be acting
the part of Diogenes, the Greek Cynic
philosopher, who despised worldly
possessions.

GUERCINO

(Giovanni Francesco Barbieri)
Italian, 1591–1666
Pope Gregory XV,
circa 1622–23
Oil on canvas
133.4 × 97.8 cm (52½ × 38½ in.)
87.PA.38

Baroque portraits of exalted sitters often
concentrate on the trappings of power
without aiming to represent character.
This picture is a remarkable exception.
Instead of merely portraying the pontiff in his official capacity, Guercino
depicted him sympathetically in the last
months of his life, worn by the cares of
office and failing health.

ORAZIO
GENTILESCHI

Italian, 1563–1639
Lot and His Daughters,
circa 1622
Oil on canvas
151.7 × 189 cm (59¼ × 72½ in.)
98.PA.10

The artist delights in contrasting Lot's drunkenness
with the heightened senses of his daughters as they
witness the destruction of Sodom by God. The graceful composition of interlocking figures, along with
the luminous harmony of colors and the rich play
of textures, characterize the elegant, poetic style that
made Gentileschi's works popular in courts across
Europe.

PIER FRANCESCO
MOLA

Italian, 1612–1666
The Vision of Saint Bruno,
circa 1660
Oil on canvas
194 × 137 cm (76⅜ × 53⅞ in.)
89.PA.4

Saint Bruno was the founder of the Carthusian order, a
monastic community committed to solitary meditation
as the most effective means of attaining union with
God. Here the saint demonstrates this hermetic ideal,
reaching to touch a vision that has appeared during
his devotions in the wilderness.

Mola won fame in Rome for his rich landscapes with
dramatic cloud formations based on Venetian examples.
In this work he also demonstrates his exceptional ability
to convey complex psychological states as he explores
one of the most important themes of Baroque art:
humanity's confrontation with the divine.

BERNARDO BELLOTTO

Italian, 1721–1780
View of the Grand Canal:
Santa Maria della Salute and
the Dogana from Campo Santa
Maria Zobenigo, circa 1740
Oil on canvas
135.5 × 232.5 cm
(53¼ × 91¼ in.)
91.PA.73

Bernardo Bellotto's precocious talent was fostered by his uncle, Canaletto (1697 – 1768), a painter famous for idealized views of his native Venice. Painted while Bellotto was still in Canaletto's studio, the *View of the Grand Canal* is an early masterpiece that demonstrates the young artist's ability to carry out a complex composition that is monumental in scale and bold in pictorial handling.

This splendid view of the Grand Canal looks from the small square, or *campo*, beside the Church of Santa Maria Zobenigo toward the opening of the canal into the great bay before Saint Mark's Square at the heart of the city. At left are a portion of the *campo* and the Palazzo Pisani-Gritti. The opposite bank is dominated by the Church of Santa Maria della Salute, the masterwork of Venetian Baroque architecture and one of the city's most famous monuments.

Other than the row of modest houses at right, demolished in the late nineteenth century, the buildings depicted in Bellotto's view remain virtually the same today. Studying the vista from the *campo* makes it clear that the painter took substantial liberty in adjusting the relationships of the structures to better suit his composition. Far more than a simple architectural record, Bellotto's painting seems to capture the grandeur of Venice at a specific moment in time, including the fleeting, magical qualities of light uniquely found there.

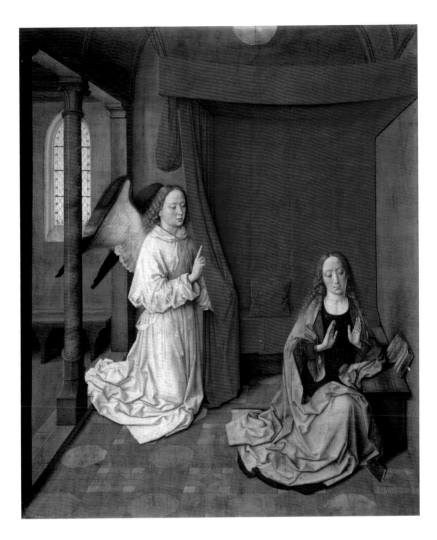

DIERIC BOUTS

Netherlandish,
circa 1415–1475
The Annunciation,
circa 1450–55
Distemper on linen
90 × 74.5 cm (35⁷⁄₁₆ × 29⅛ in.)
85.PA.24

This painting represents the Incarnation, or conception of Christ, which occurred when the Archangel Gabriel announced to the Virgin Mary, "You shall conceive and bear a son, and you shall give him the name of Jesus" (Luke 1:31). Mary, seated on the ground to indicate her humility, responds with a gesture conveying her acknowledgment of the miracle and acceptance of God's will. Bouts created a composition of surprising simplicity, minimizing symbolic detail to establish a mood of hushed solemnity. This image was executed in an equally austere technique. Thin washes of pigment in animal glue were applied to fine linen to give the scene a delicate, luminous quality. This was the first scene in an altarpiece relating the Life of Christ; the final scene, *The Resurrection,* is in the Norton Simon Museum, Pasadena.

MARTIN SCHONGAUER

German, 1450/53–1491
*Madonna and Child in
a Window*, circa 1485–90
Oil on panel
16.5 × 11 cm (6½ × 4¾ in.)
97.PB.23

Madonna and Child in a Window is one of only seven known paintings by Martin Schongauer, who was renowned as a printmaker. A vigorous linearity animates this devotional work in which the Virgin appears as the Window to Heaven. This tiny panel showcases Schongauer's superb ability to convincingly render materials, such as the jeweled crown and scepter held by the angel, as well as the delicate features of the Virgin and the inquisitive Child.

**MASTER OF
THE SAINT
BARTHOLOMEW
ALTARPIECE**

Netherlandish, active in
Cologne, circa 1480–1510
*The Meeting of the Three
Kings with David and Isaiah*
(recto)
The Assumption of the Virgin
(verso), before 1480
Oil and gold leaf on panel
62.8 × 71.2 cm (24¼ × 28⅛ in.)
96.PB.16

German Renaissance masters responded to Netherlandish painting with their own particular narrative and
graphic force. In *The Meeting of the Three Kings*, the
Magi and their retinues converge at Golgotha on their
journey to Bethlehem. In the foreground, the Old Testament prophets David (left) and Isaiah (right) clasp
scrolling banners foretelling the Adoration of the Magi.
The reverse of this panel illustrates the Assumption of
the Virgin (not shown). This well-preserved work
probably came from the wing of a lost altarpiece dedicated to the Virgin.

JAN GOSSAERT

(called Mabuse)
Netherlandish, circa 1478–1532
Francisco de los Cobos
y Molina, circa 1530–32
Oil on panel
43.8 × 33.7 cm (17¼ × 13¼ in.)
88.PB.43

The most accomplished Flemish painter of his generation, Gossaert combined keen observation of form,
facile rendering of surface textures, and psychological
insight to create portraits remarkable for their strong
physical presence. This one probably represents
Francisco de los Cobos, a major Spanish patron who
was the powerful secretary and chief financial adviser
to Emperor Charles V (reigned 1519–1556).

JAN BRUEGHEL THE ELDER

Flemish, 1568–1625
The Entry of the Animals
into Noah's Ark, 1613
Oil on panel
54.6 × 83.8 cm (21½ × 33 in.)
92.PB.82

This is the first of a group of Paradise landscapes developed by Brueghel, the most important Flemish landscape painter working at the dawn of the Baroque era.
In this episode from the story of Noah's ark (Genesis
68), Brueghel celebrates the beauty and variety of
God's creations. His encyclopedic representation of
animals reflects the new interest in natural history.
While court painter to the Archduke Albert in Brussels,
he studied the exotic animals and birds in the royal
menagerie. This painting exemplifies Brueghel's meticulous attention to detail and use of vivid colors.

PETER PAUL RUBENS

Flemish, 1577–1640
The Entombment, circa 1612
Oil on canvas
131 × 130.2 cm (51⅝ × 51¼ in.)
93.PA.9

Rubens was a devout Catholic, and his paintings give tangible form to the main concerns of his religion. This powerful work was carefully composed to focus devotion on Jesus Christ's sacrifice and suffering. The head of Christ, frozen in the agony of death, is turned to confront the observer directly. Rubens also compels us to regard the gaping wound in Christ's side, placing it at the center of the canvas. The viewer is obliged to join the mourners, whose grief is focused in the Virgin Mary, weeping as she implores heaven.

Rubens also introduces symbolic elements that reflect the theological and political concerns of the Counter-Reformation in the early seventeenth century. Thus, the slab on which the body is placed suggests an altar, while the sheaf of wheat alludes to the bread of the Eucharist, the equivalent of Christ's body in the Mass. At this time the Roman Church was defending the mystery of Transubstantiation, the belief in the real presence of the body of Christ in the Eucharist, against Protestant criticism.

ANTHONY
VAN DYCK

Flemish, 1599–1641
Agostino Pallavicini,
circa 1621
Oil on canvas
216 × 141 cm (85⅛ × 55½ in.)
68.PA.2

Shortly after arriving in Italy, Van Dyck is known to
have painted Agostino Pallavicini dressed in the
robes of an ambassador to the pope. The sketchy cur-
tain behind the sitter here bears the Pallavicini coat
of arms, and his dramatic robes surely were intended
for ceremonial duties. Van Dyck emulated his master
Rubens's rich and dramatic painting style but brought
to portraiture a unique aristocratic refinement that
transformed the genre.

JOACHIM WTEWAEL

Dutch, 1566–1638
*Mars and Venus Surprised by
Vulcan*, circa 1606–10
Oil on copper
20.25 × 15.5 cm (8 × 6⅛ in.)
83.PC.274

In this small painting Wtewael has depicted a scene from
Ovid's *Metamorphoses* (4:171–189) with appropriate
raucous humor. As Vulcan (at the bottom right) draws
his forged net from the bed, the lovers Mars and Venus
(Vulcan's wife) reel back. Cupid and Apollo raise the
canopy for a peek, and a gleeful Mercury (wearing a
winged cap) looks up to Diana in the clouds at the right.
Saturn (holding a sickle) and Jupiter crane their necks
to behold the embarrassed adulterers. The rhythmically
paired heroic nude figures show Wtewael at the height
of his inventive powers as a Mannerist artist.

The use of copper as a support for paintings was
especially widespread during the late sixteenth and
early seventeenth centuries. The very hard and polished
surface was well suited for the present picture, since
it allowed for subtler gradations of tone and greater intensity of color than canvas.

This tiny cabinet picture may have been painted for
the private enjoyment of a connoisseur familiar with
Ovid's text and capable of appreciating both the artist's
skill and the significance of the painting's symbolic
details. It was probably the painting commissioned by
Joan van Weely, a jeweler from Amsterdam.

HENDRICK
TER BRUGGHEN

Dutch, 1588–1629
Bacchante with an Ape, 1627
Oil on canvas
102.9 × 90.1 cm
(40½ × 35½ in.)
84.PA.5

This devotee of Bacchus, with her fruit, nuts, and ape (a symbol of appetite or gluttony), may represent the sense of taste. Caravaggio had set the fashion for half-length figures representing the senses in Rome at the turn of the century, and his works certainly influenced ter Brugghen's both in type and style. Coming from a Catholic city in largely Protestant Holland, ter Brugghen was one of the few Dutch artists to visit Italy in an era of religious controversy and so became instrumental in the spread of new Italian styles to the North. The lively, unidealized portrayal of the model and the sculptural modeling of the flesh in darks and lights are characteristic of the Caravaggesque style ter Brugghen adopted while in Rome (1604–14) and carried back to his native Utrecht.

PIETER JANSZ. SAENREDAM

Dutch, 1597–1665
The Interior of the Church of Saint Bavo, Haarlem, 1628
Oil on panel
38.5 × 47.5 cm (15¼ × 18¼ in.)
85.PB.225

Pieter Saenredam, the great renovator of architecture painting in the Netherlands, transformed the idealized, artificial perspective of earlier pictures done mostly by Flemish artists. By minimizing anecdote and adopting an unusually low viewpoint, Saenredam concentrated on the depiction of light, color, and space in monumental buildings.

The Interior of the Church of Saint Bavo, Haarlem is the earliest known painting by Saenredam. It is the first of twelve paintings of the interior of this church—one of the finest Gothic buildings in Holland—that he painted between 1628 and 1660. Saenredam conceived his views of church interiors with the help of detailed, on-the-spot studies, extensive measurements, and perspective drawings. In this painting, the artist transcends mere architectural portraiture by merging two distinct views of the church: from the north transept straight ahead into the south transept, and to the east, into the choir. Different shades of white paint—ranging from bluish-white to creamy yellow—suggest the northern and southern light shining into the building. Remarkably, Saenredam substituted an altarpiece for the doors in the church's south transept and included a stained glass window with a depiction of the Immaculate Conception. These elements suggest a Catholic commission for this painting.

REMBRANDT
HARMENSZ.
VAN RIJN

Dutch, 1606–1669
The Abduction of Europa, 1632
Oil on panel
62.2 × 77 cm (24½ × 30⁵⁄₁₆ in.)
95.PB.7

Rembrandt regarded history painting—the portrayal
and interpretation of great stories of the past—as
his most important activity. During his early years in
Amsterdam he turned to classical mythology for subjects such as *The Abduction of Europa*, which derives
from Ovid's *Metamorphoses*. In it Jupiter, the king of
the gods, has transformed himself into a beautiful white
bull in order to seduce Europa, the princess of Tyre.
Beguiled, she climbs onto the bull's back and is spirited
across the sea to the continent that will one day bear
her name. Rembrandt evokes the poetry of Ovid's tale
by showing Europa as she "trembles with fear and
looks back at the receding shore, holding fast a horn . . .
her fluttering garments stream[ing] . . . in the wind."
He enriches the narrative through his vivid characterization of emotion and accentuates the drama by contrasting the shadowed immobility of the land with the
shimmering movement of the sea and the sky.

REMBRANDT
HARMENSZ.
VAN RIJN

Dutch, 1606–1669
*Daniel and Cyrus Before
the Idol Bel*, 1633
Oil on panel
23.4 × 30.1 cm (9¼ × 11⅞ in.)
95.PB.15

Rembrandt took this ancient detective story from
the apocryphal Book of Daniel. It tells of Daniel's
unmasking of idolatry at the court of Babylon, where
he had become a confidant of King Cyrus of Persia.
When Cyrus asked his trusted adviser why he did not
honor the deity Bel, Daniel replied that he worshiped
the living God, not an idol. The king insisted that Bel
too was a living god, indicating the offerings of food
and wine he provided for Bel's consumption each night.
In this rendering, Daniel gently points out that bronze
statues don't eat. The worried face of one of the priests
confirms that Daniel is on to something, and Cyrus
begins to realize that he may have been duped. Later in
the story, Daniel secretly spreads ashes on the floor
of the temple, and, the next morning, the footprints of
the priests and their families reveal the truth.

Rembrandt evokes a mood of mystery with flickering light and the partial view of the monumental idol.
He then tells the story with gesture and expression,
emphasizing the contrast between the large, powerful
Cyrus and the small, humble Daniel. Created the year
after *The Abduction of Europa* (see previous entry), this
work shows Rembrandt's evolution toward the more
concise and dramatically focused compositions of his
mature style. Both paintings demonstrate the humanity
at the heart of Rembrandt's genius as a storyteller.

REMBRANDT HARMENSZ. VAN RIJN

Dutch, 1606–1669
An Old Man in Military Costume, circa 1630–31
Oil on panel
66 × 50.8 cm (26 × 20 in.)
78.PB.246

From the beginning of his career, Rembrandt was occupied with historical subjects. He soon took up a related genre, which he made his own: studies of individual costumed figures.

Such works as *An Old Man in Military Costume* are not primarily portraits but rather studies in which Rembrandt explored the human condition.

PHILIPS KONINCK

Dutch, 1619–1688
Panoramic Landscape, 1665
Oil on canvas
138 × 167 cm (54½ × 65½ in.)
85.PA.32

Koninck's expansive view, like Rembrandt's drawings and prints of landscapes (see p. 168), combines real and imagined elements to create the illusion of sweeping space seen from a great height.

REMBRANDT HARMENSZ. VAN RIJN

Dutch, 1606–1669
Saint Bartholomew, 1661
Oil on canvas
86.5 × 75.5 cm (34⅛ × 29¾ in.)
71.PA.15

Rembrandt's subject has been identified as Saint Bartholomew by virtue of the knife—the instrument of his martyrdom—gripped in his right hand, but the actual sitter may have been one of the artist's friends or neighbors in Amsterdam. Rembrandt painted several deeply moving studies of such men in the guise of saints and apostles in the early 1660s. Somberly colored and expressively painted, the *Saint Bartholomew* is an examination of age and introspection. The momentary distraction of the *Old Man in Military Costume* (see p. 120) has given way to the saint's profound absorption; his thoughts are far removed from the present. During the thirty years between the *Old Man* and this painting, Rembrandt's style also shifted from concern for surface effects to a probing analysis of form and structure.

JAN VAN DE
CAPPELLE

Dutch, 1626–1679
*Shipping in a Calm at Flushing
with a States-General Yacht
Firing a Salute*, 1649
Oil on panel
69.7 × 92.2 cm (27⅛ × 36¼ in.)
96.PB.7

In the mid-seventeenth century, when the Dutch
Republic had reached its height of power as a global
trading empire, its domination of the seas found expression in the nascent specialization of marine painting. In
1649, Jan van de Cappelle and Simon de Vlieger changed
the course of Dutch seascapes with an innovation
known as the "parade" picture, which showed grand
ships convening for special occasions under towering,
cloud-filled skies.

In *Shipping in a Calm* a stately yacht fires a salute,
which announces the arrival of a dignitary, who is
conveyed to shore in a launch at right. Unaffected by
the shot, porpoises glide peacefully through the
calm waters. They were known to frequent Flushing
(Vlissingen), the busy port used by the Dutch East
India Company, which was frequently portrayed in van
de Cappelle's paintings.

As one of his earliest known signed and dated
works, this painting displays van de Cappelle's highly
developed style and remarkable technical virtuosity.
The painter demonstrates an accomplished graphic
handling of form in the detailed ships, rigging, and sails,
and his mastery of optical effects in the treatment of
reflections in the water. This dramatic avenue of ships
framing an infinite vista of the sea is a pioneering contribution to the genre of marine painting.

JAN STEEN

Dutch, 1626–1679
The Drawing Lesson,
circa 1665
Oil on panel
49.3 × 41 cm (19⅛ × 16¼ in.)
83.PB.388

FRANS VAN MIERIS
THE ELDER

Dutch, 1635–1681
An Allegory of Painting, 1661
Oil on copper
12.5 × 8.5 cm (5 × 3½ in.)
82.PC.136

These two compositions are both allegories of the painter's art. The Steen
shows the interior of a painter's studio,
cluttered with symbolic objects, while
the painter, his apprentice, and a young
woman concentrate on correcting a
drawing. Several of the symbolic objects
in *The Drawing Lesson* also appear as
attributes of Pictura, a personification
of the art of painting. Along with her
palette, brushes, and statue, this figure
wears a mask hung on a chain around
her neck. The mask may be an emblem
of deceit or illusion (the painter creates
an illusion of reality), or it may refer
to the dramatic arts (like the dramatist,
the painter must invent and "stage"
convincing scenes).

PAULUS POTTER

Dutch, 1625–1654
The Piebald Horse,
circa 1650–54
Oil on canvas
49.5 × 45 cm (19½ × 17¹¹⁄₁₆ in.)
88.PA.87

GERARD TER
BORCH

Dutch, 1617–1681
Horse Stable, circa 1654
Oil on panel
45.3 × 53.5 cm
(17¹³⁄₁₆ × 21¹⁄₁₆ in.)
86.PB.631

A horse was valuable
property in seventeenth-
century Holland. Both of
these paintings reflect
the pride the prosperous
Dutch took in their
costly livestock. Potter,
the most successful ani-
mal painter of his time,
painted this magnificent
piebald horse as a monu-
mental creature, attesting
to its nobility. The horseman in the background,
returning with his groom
and dogs to his country
house, may be the ani-
mal's owner. Ter Borch's
Horse Stable is roughly
contemporary. A fine
riding horse is repre-
sented in a barn, tended
by a man dressed in
distinctly middle-class
attire, as is the woman
at the right. This subject
was highly unusual for
ter Borch, normally
a painter of sophisticated
genre scenes and portraits.

Jan van Huysum

Dutch, 1682–1749
Vase of Flowers, 1722
Oil on panel
79.5 × 61 cm (31¼ × 24 in.)
82.PB.70

Ambrosius Bosschaert the Elder

Dutch, 1573–1621
Flower Still Life, 1614
Oil on copper
28.6 × 38.1 cm (11¼ × 15 in.)
83.PC.386

The mania for cultivating flowers in Baroque Europe fostered the development and popularity of flower painters. One of the earliest of these specialists, Ambrosius Bosschaert the Elder, has grouped flowers from different seasons — roses, tulips, forget-me-nots, cyclamen, a violet, and a hyacinth — along with insects equally beautiful and short-lived. Jan van Huysum's bouquet of a century later includes several of the same flowers and insects as well as a bird's nest. Both painters celebrated the decorative qualities of their subjects but also intended to provoke serious reflection on the transience of life and beauty.

Georges de La Tour

French, 1593–1652
The Musicians' Brawl,
circa 1625–30
Oil on canvas
85.7 × 141 cm (33¾ × 55½ in.)
72.PA.28

This early La Tour composition shows a scuffle between two beggar musicians. Scholars have suggested that the two troupes are fighting for possession of a lucrative street corner; that the scene was taken from comedic theater; and that the man in velvet is unmasking the false blindness of the hurdy-gurdy player by squirting lemon juice in his eye. La Tour illuminates this frieze of beggars with a cold, overhead light. His strange palette, attention to unusual textures such as the wrinkled skin of the aged beggar, and the detached treatment of characters made La Tour one of the most original and enigmatic artists of the seventeenth century.

NICOLAS POUSSIN

French, 1594–1665
The Holy Family, circa 1651
Oil on canvas
100.6 × 132.4 cm
(39⅝ × 52⅛ in.)
81.PA.43
(Owned jointly with the
Norton Simon Art
Foundation, Pasadena)

The traditional Holy Family, which includes the Virgin
and Child with Saint Joseph, has here been extended
to include the youthful Saint John the Baptist with
his mother, Saint Elizabeth. Framed by the passive figures of their parents, the holy children reach out in
a lively embrace. Six putti bearing a basket of flowers,
a ewer, a towel, and a basin of water may prefigure
Saint John's later baptism of Christ. Painted in Poussin's
late classicizing style, *The Holy Family* reflects his
study of Raphael and antique sculpture. It exemplifies
Poussin's intellectual approach to painting, his insis-
tence on harmony among all parts of the composition,
and his concentration on the ideal and the abstract.

NICOLAS POUSSIN

French, 1594–1665
Landscape with a Calm,
1650–51
Oil on canvas
97 × 131.5 cm (39 × 52¾ in.)
97.PA.60

A Calm culminates Poussin's development of the
"heroic landscape," a view of nature idealized through
the application of classical models and optical princi-
ples. Painted as a pendant to *A Storm* (Musée des Beaux
Arts, Rouen) for the Lyonaise merchant Jean Pointel,
A Calm is without literary subject. One of Poussin's
purest landscapes, its meaning hinges on the artist's
ability to capture the essence of nature's order. Indeed,
the pellucid harmonies of *A Calm* led Poussin's biographer Félibien to exclaim that in it, "Nature seems to
paint herself in reflections."

Jean-François de Troy

French, 1679–1752
Before the Ball, 1735
Oil on canvas
81.8 × 65 cm (32⅛ × 25⁹/₁₆ in.)
84.PA.668

De Troy, a painter of historical, religious, and mythological subjects, is
best remembered for his invention of the
tableau de mode showing elegant company in fashionable interiors. Inspired
by the *fêtes galantes* of Watteau and his
circle and by seventeenth-century Dutch
genre paintings, de Troy depicts a group
of gallants preparing for a masked ball.
Their lavish dress and the fine furniture
add to the opulence of the setting. The
mood of hushed expectancy is enhanced
by the flickering candlelight that illuminates the room.

Maurice-Quentin de La Tour

French, 1704–1788
Gabriel Bernard de Rieux,
1739–41
Pastel and gouache on paper
mounted on canvas
Unframed: 200 × 150 cm
(79 × 59 in.)
Framed: 317.5 × 223.5 cm
(125 × 88 in.)
94.PC.39

Maurice-Quentin de La Tour was the most sought-after
portraitist of his day. He worked exclusively in pastel,
producing likenesses of the nobility and the wealthy
middle class that were acclaimed both for their technical mastery and for their brilliant verisimilitude. After
seeing the portrait of Gabriel Bernard de Rieux at the
Salon of 1741, a viewer wrote, "It is a miraculous work,
it is like a piece of Dresden china, it cannot possibly
be a mere pastel." The fine differentiation between textures, the play of light over reflective surfaces, and
the overall high degree of finish were qualities expected
from oils, but they were extraordinarily difficult
to achieve in frangible pastels. The work was La Tour's
successful challenge to the prestigious medium of oil.

This monumental full-length portrait, still in its
original massive gilt frame, transcends the intimate
conventions of pastel. During his long career La Tour
did only one other like it, the portrait of Madame
de Pompadour now in the Musée du Louvre, Paris.
The Getty Museum's portrait, assembled from separate
sheets of paper laid on canvas, shows Gabriel Bernard
de Rieux (1687–1745) dressed in the robes of his
office as President of the Second Court of Inquiry in
the Parliament of Paris.

JEAN-BAPTISTE
GREUZE

French, 1725–1805
The Laundress, 1761
Oil on canvas
40.6 × 32.4 cm
(16 × 12⅞ in.)
83.PA.387

*Cimon and Pero: "Roman
Charity,"* circa 1767
Oil on canvas
62.9 × 79.4 cm
(24¾ × 31¼ in.)
99.PA.24

At the Salon of 1761 the *Laundress* beguiled critics like
Denis Diderot, who commented, "this little laundress
is charming, but she's a rascal I wouldn't trust an inch."
By 1767 Greuze harbored higher ambitions than success
as a genre painter. The large oil sketch of "Roman
Charity" is a rare example from his subsequent two-
year preoccupation with historical subjects. Both paintings reveal Greuze's graphic facility with the brush,
his attention to sensuous paint textures, and his remarkable ability—achieved through careful life-studies—
to capture human emotions ranging from a young
laundress's coy appraisal to an old man's desperation.

JEAN-HONORÉ
FRAGONARD

French, 1732–1806
The Fountain of Love,
1780s
Oil on canvas
62.2 × 51.4 cm (24½ × 20¼ in.)
99.PA.30

Fragonard, best known for delightful Rococo images, responded to the later Neoclassical movement with his own dreamy, moonlit vision of antiquity. In *The Fountain of Love*, luminous effects and fluid brushwork bring softness to figures based on classical sculpture.

The focal point of a poetic allegory of the progress of love, the fountain brings forth the waters from which couples drink and fall in love. During the eighteenth century, artists treated the Fountain of Love as a genre subject, with lovers in contemporary dress engaged in flirtation. But here, Fragonard returns the allegory to its classical origins, imbuing it with the rush of those thrilling moments of the first taste of love.

JACQUES-LOUIS DAVID

French, 1748–1825
*Suzanne Le Peletier
de Saint-Fargeau*, 1804
Oil on canvas
60.5 × 49.5 cm (23¾ × 19½ in.)
97.PA.36

Despite the demanding obligations of his new position as Napoleon's First Painter, David created this intimate portrait of Suzanne Le Peletier, the daughter of a revolutionary martyr. Posed almost casually, Suzanne gazes calmly and frankly out at the viewer—probably intended to be her fiancé. Rapid, loose brushstrokes describe Suzanne's tousled dark curls and the folds of her simple, stylish clothing.

JACQUES-LOUIS DAVID

French, 1748–1825
*The Farewell of Telemachus
and Eucharis*, 1818
Oil on canvas
87.2 × 103 cm (34½ × 40½ in.)
87.PA.27

During the final decade of his life, which he spent in voluntary exile in Brussels, David created a series of innovative mythological paintings with themes of erotic entanglements. In *The Farewell*, filial duty requires Telemachus to abandon the nymph Eucharis to search for his missing father, Odysseus. Elegantly interlacing the figures of the lovers, David played his perfection of line and form against Flemish-inspired color harmonies of reds, blues, and cool flesh tones.

THÉODORE
GÉRICAULT

French, 1791–1824
*The Race of the Riderless
Horses*, 1817
Oil on paper laid on canvas
19.9 × 29.1 cm (7¹³/₁₆ × 11⁷/₁₆ in.)
85.PC.406

Géricault devoted much of his year in Rome (1816–17)
to planning a monumental painting of the race of
the riderless horses, the climax of the Roman Carnival
season. The furious struggle between lunging animals
and their handlers at the start of the race may symbolize
the Romantic artist's search for a balance between
his own passions and his need for professional discipline.

THÉODORE
GÉRICAULT

French, 1791–1824
Three Lovers, 1817–20
Oil on canvas
22.5 × 29.8 cm (8⅞ × 11¾ in.)
95.PA.72

Drawn curtains and a statue of Venus frame a dramatically lit interior. Within it a couple, clothed in contemporary dress, make love while a nude, reclining woman
watches them. Géricault's direct presentation of an
erotic subject, without moralizing or sentimental justi-
fication, is unprecedented. His translation of a contemporary event into a timeless setting makes modern
life appropriate for high art. The free technique of
this small-scale, independent finished sketch unites the
emotional immediacy of the subject with the dramatic
spontaneity of the artist's touch.

THÉODORE
GÉRICAULT

French, 1791–1824
Portrait Study, circa 1818–19
Oil on canvas
46.7 × 38 cm (18⅜ × 15 in.)
85.PA.407

This portrait may represent Joseph, the professional artist's model who posed for Géricault's masterpiece *The Raft of the Medusa* (Paris, Musée du Louvre), completed in 1819. A haunting character study never used in the larger work, this portrait belongs to an important group of paintings and drawings of African men by Géricault.

JEAN-FRANÇOIS
MILLET

French, 1814–1875
*Louise-Antoinette
Feuardent*, 1841
Oil on canvas
73.3 × 60.6 cm (28⅞ × 23⅞ in.)
95.PA.67

Before his move to Barbizon and international success as a painter of peasant life, Jean-François Millet earned his living as a portraitist. Millet depicted Louise-Antoinette Feuardent in the middle of his two-year stay in the Norman city of Cherbourg. The young wife of Millet's lifelong friend, Félix-Bienaimé Feuardent, a clerk in the city library, is portrayed with carefully deliberated simplicity. The setting is plain, the costume unpretentious, and the mood contained. This, one of Millet's most tender and moving portraits, captures the understated virtue of a modern woman from the provinces.

JEAN-FRANÇOIS MILLET

French, 1814–1875
Man with a Hoe, 1860–62
Oil on canvas
80 × 99 cm (31½ × 39 in.)
85.PA.114

When Millet first exhibited *Man with a Hoe* at the Salon of 1863, it raised a storm of controversy that lasted well into the twentieth century. The artist intended his image of an exhausted peasant to represent the dignity and strange beauty of manual labor. By contrasting the bent, awkward figure with the richly painted, broken earth of the field, Millet was calling attention to the costs and benefits of agrarian life. The division of the foreground into distinct patches of stony, thorny terrain and cultivated earth graphically portrays the results of the peasant's toil. However, the starkness of the scene and harsh characterization of the peasant were attacked by most of the critics who reviewed the 1863 exhibition. Moreover, since it concluded a long series of similar subjects Millet painted during a decade of heated public debate over the fate of the peasant in French society, *Man with a Hoe* was taken by some to represent the socialist position on the laboring poor. In response to claims that his painting was both ugly and politically radical, Millet responded, "Some tell me that I deny the charms of the country. I find more than charms, I find infinite glories. . . . But I see as well, in the plain, the steaming horses at work, and in a rocky place a man, all worn out, whose 'Han!' has been heard since morning, and who tries to straighten himself for a moment and breathe. The drama is surrounded by beauty."

PIERRE-AUGUSTE
RENOIR

French, 1841–1919
La Promenade, 1870
Oil on canvas
81.3 × 65 cm (32 × 25½ in.)
89.PA.41

Renoir's promenading couple heads for the undergrowth. Although the subject owes its inspiration to Watteau, Courbet, and Monet, the technique of using different brushwork for different purposes was entirely Renoir's. Thus he defined the white dress with long, flowing strokes but created the landscape with short touches that skitter and dance on the surface. Light, atmosphere, and the diagonal movements of the lovers unify the composition. The artist's vigorous enjoyment of pleasure — both amorous and painterly — animates every aspect of this early Impressionist work.

PIERRE-AUGUSTE RENOIR

French, 1841–1919
Albert Cahen d'Anvers, 1881
Oil on canvas
79.8 × 63.7 cm (31⁷⁄₁₆ × 25⅛ in.)
88.PA.133

In the late 1870s and early 1880s Renoir earned most of his income from portraiture. The solid monumentality of his portrait of the orchestral composer Albert Cahen d'Anvers (1846–1903) is typical of these works and reflects Renoir's growing interest in Renaissance art some ten years after he painted *La Promenade* (see p. 136). The young man's vivid coloring probably inspired Renoir to base his composition on contrasting reds and blues.

ÉDOUARD MANET

French, 1832–1883
The Rue Mosnier with Flags, 1878
Oil on canvas
65.5 × 81 cm (25¼ × 31¼ in.)
89.PA.71

On June 30, 1878, the day of a national celebration, Manet painted two canvases of his street with its decoration of flags. This deceptively casual rendering, executed as late afternoon shadows advanced down the rue Mosnier, captures the scene with brilliant economy. Virtuoso brushwork describes the scene with minimal fuss and maximum effect. Manet's commitment to subjects from modern life makes this painting more than an urban landscape, however; the poignant juxtaposition of the *quartier*'s one-legged veteran with elegant façades and carriages along the street suggests the inequities of life in the new urban environment.

EDGAR DEGAS

French, 1834–1917
Waiting, circa 1882
Pastel on paper
48.2 × 61 cm (19 × 24 in.)
83.GG.219
(Owned jointly with the
Norton Simon Art
Foundation, Pasadena)

Unlike his contemporaries the Impressionists, Degas arranged his subjects into compositions of great formal beauty laden with emotional power. In this pastel Degas may have intended the juxtaposed figures on the bench to contrast the brilliant, artificial world of the theater with the drabness of everyday life. If the suggestion is correct that the scene shows a dancer and her mother from the provinces awaiting an audition at the Paris Opera, then a contrast between the ephemeral glamour of the opera dancer and the dreary respectability of the provincial woman may also be implied. Each figure is absorbed in her own thoughts, yet they share a sense of tension and anticipation.

CLAUDE MONET

French, 1840–1926
*Wheatstacks, Snow Effect,
Morning*, 1891
Oil on canvas
65 × 100 cm (25½ × 39¼ in.)
95.PA.63

Monet's desire to capture fleeting effects led him later in the 1890s to explore the concept of "series painting." *Wheatstacks* is one of the earliest and most tightly structured paintings in a series of thirty canvases. Its brilliant, variegated palette and richly worked surface reveal Monet's intense efforts in the studio. Remarkably, both *Wheatstacks* and *Sunrise* are unlined and, as a result, preserve the crispness of Monet's brushwork and the freshness of the painted surface.

CLAUDE MONET

French, 1840–1926
Sunrise, 1873
Oil on canvas
49 × 60 cm (19¼ × 23½ in.)
98.PA.164

A keen pleasure in evoking the interplay of light, atmosphere, and water shaped Monet's approach to painting landscape. Early in his career, in the spring of 1873, Monet traveled to the bustling port of Le Havre. There he painted *Sunrise* and six other early-morning views of the harbor. The broken brushwork of these scenes appeared to lack "finish" and were derisively called "Impressionist" by critics, heralding the beginning of an artistic movement.

PAUL CÉZANNE

French, 1839 – 1906
Still Life with Apples,
1893 – 94
Oil on canvas
65.5 × 81.5 cm (25¼ × 32⅛ in.)
96.PA.8

Still life held an important, even obsessive, position throughout Cézanne's career. The immobility and long-lasting nature of the objects he chose allowed him the time and control to pursue his pictorial analysis of the relationship between space and object, between visual experience and pictorial rendering.

Still Life with Apples is an elegantly composed, powerfully rendered image of familiar objects. The graceful rhythms created by the swinging black arabesques of the blue cloth, the looping rattan, and the swelling curves of the pots and fruit are played against the strong horizontals and verticals of the composition. Cézanne self-consciously integrates the objects to lock the composition together; a black arabesque "escapes" from the blue cloth to capture an apple in the center; the sinuous curves of the blue ginger pot's rattan straps are visually continued in the bottle. The green of the vase is counterbalanced by the red and yellow apples in this predominantly blue painting. His careful orchestration results in an image of balance, stasis, and control. Cézanne's professed goals "to do Poussin again after nature" and to make of Impressionism "something solid and enduring" are here achieved in the classical stability of this masterful work.

PAUL CÉZANNE

French, 1839–1906
*Young Italian Woman
at a Table*, circa 1895–1900
Oil on canvas
91.7 × 73.3 cm (36⅛ × 28⅞ in.)
99.PA.40

Paul Cézanne has been celebrated as the greatest figure of the Impressionist generation, as the artist who laid the foundations of Cubism, and as the father of abstract art and the modern movement. His best known and most influential work dates from the last decades of his life and unites an objective recording of the artist's visual experience with controlled, unified structure and monumentalizing grandeur. *Young Italian Woman* reveals Cézanne at his most enigmatic and poignant; though the woman's physical presence is compelling, her withheld thoughts and emotions create a mood of profound melancholy.

JEAN-ÉTIENNE LIOTARD

Swiss, 1702–1789
*Maria Frederike van
Reede-Athlone at Seven
Years of Age*, 1755–56
Pastel on vellum
57.2 × 47 cm (22½ × 18½ in.)
83.PC.273

Liotard strived to record three-
dimensional objects faithfully, a technique he called "deception painting."
His definition of volume through subtle
gradations of color and his brilliant
description of surface textures create
the startling realism that makes his work
unique. Here he captures the alert intelligence of a seven-year-old girl from an
aristocratic Dutch family with amazing
immediacy. By choosing a plain background, Liotard focuses attention on
the sitter, her clothing, and her pet dog.
He suggests an enigmatic shyness on
the part of the girl, whose averted eyes
imply a complex personality about to
bloom. The child's refined elegance
contrasts with the eager curiosity of the
dog, who stares at the viewer. Utilizing
the difficult medium of pastel, Liotard
masterfully evoked both the physicality
and psychology of his subject.

THOMAS GAINSBOROUGH

English, 1727–1788
James Christie, 1778
Oil on canvas
126 × 102 cm (49⅝ × 40⅛ in.)
70.PA.16

James Christie, founder of the London
auction house that still bears his name, is
depicted as if attending one of his own
sales. Much praised at the time of its
exhibition at the Royal Academy, the
portrait epitomizes Rococo elegance and
grace. The style's characteristic arabesques are found in Christie's relaxed
pose, in the tree and foliage of the
Gainsborough landscape he leans
against, in the gilt frame of the painting
behind it, and in the artist's accomplished, free handling of paint throughout the composition.

JOSEPH MALLORD
WILLIAM TURNER

English, 1775–1851
*Van Tromp, going about to
please his Masters, Ships a
Sea, getting a Good Wetting,*
1844
Oil on canvas
91.4 × 121.9 cm (36 × 48 in.)
93.PA.32

Turner united two of his passions, the sea and Holland,
in this painting, which he first exhibited at the Royal
Academy in 1844. It depicts a combination of events
from the lives of two men, Admiral Maarten Har-
pertszoon Tromp (1598–1653) and his son Cornelius
(1629–1691). Both earned renown for their naval
victories against British and Spanish fleets during the
height of Dutch seafaring power.

CASPAR DAVID
FRIEDRICH

German, 1774–1840
A Walk at Dusk,
circa 1830–35
Oil on canvas
33.3 × 43.7 cm (13⅛ × 17⁷⁄₁₆ in.)
93.PA.14

Caspar David Friedrich was a leading figure of the
German Romantic movement. He is noted for his
deeply personal religious imagery in which landscapes
and natural phenomena serve as metaphors for the
most profound human experiences and sentiments.

A Walk at Dusk shows an isolated figure—dressed
as a scholar and perhaps intended as a self-portrait—
contemplating a prehistoric grave with its implicit
message of death's inevitability.

EL GRECO

(Doménikos
Theotokópoulos)
Greek, 1541–1614
Christ on the Cross,
circa 1600–10
Oil on canvas
82.6 × 51.6 cm (32½ × 20⁵⁄₁₆)
2000.40

Painting in the fervent religious climate of Counter-
Reformation Spain, El Greco developed a style unique for
its hallucinatory spiritual intensity. This small-scale work
intended for private devotion is an excellent example of
the popular "living Christ" theme. The crucified Christ is
set dramatically against a turbulent, pitch-black sky shot
through with incandescent bursts of light. Christ gazes
calmly heavenward, and his languid, attenuated body,
modeled in flickering silvery light, seems to rise vertigi-
nously above the spectral landscape, suggesting the ultimate triumph of faith over death.

FRANCISCO JOSÉ DE
GOYA Y LUCIENTES

Spanish, 1746–1828
Bullfight, Suerte de Varas,
1824
Oil on canvas
50 × 61 cm (19½ × 24 in.)
93.PA.1

This work is Goya's final painted essay on the theme of the bullfight, a subject that he popularized and that recurs throughout his career. His passion for the sport is here overlaid with horror at the abusive tactics that emerged when bullfighting was considered to be in decline, late in his life.

A horde of men and horses stands in opposition to a lone bull, their battle plan in disarray as the bull has reduced their grim determination and their numbers. Wounded and weakened, the bull is presented not as a fierce, unbridled force of nature, but as a noble beast before the rabble. His very presence in the ring assures his death, but he has nonetheless won.

An inscription on the back of the canvas identifies this work as a gift, painted in Paris during the summer of 1824, for Goya's friend and compatriot in exile Joaquín María Ferrer. Goya had only recently left his native land, at age seventy-eight, worried over possible censorship and oppression following Ferdinand VII's return to the Spanish throne in 1823.

VINCENT
VAN GOGH

Dutch, 1853–1890
Irises, 1889
Oil on canvas
71 × 93 cm (28 × 36⅝ in.)
90.PA.20

Van Gogh painted *Irises* in the garden of the asylum at Saint-Rémy, where he was recuperating from a severe attack of mental illness. Although he considered the work more a study than a finished picture, it was exhibited at the Salon des Indépendants in September 1889. Its energy and theme—the regenerative powers of the earth—express the artist's deeply held belief in the divinity of art and nature. However, the painting's vivid color contrasts, powerful brushwork, and frieze-like composition reflect van Gogh's study of other artists, notably Paul Gauguin (French, 1848–1903) and the Japanese master Hokusai (1760–1849).

LAWRENCE
ALMA TADEMA

Dutch/English, 1836–1912
Spring, 1894
Oil on canvas
178.4 × 80 cm (70¼ × 31½ in.)
72.PA.3

Born in Holland, in 1870 Alma Tadema moved as a successful artist to London, where he became a British citizen, a member of the Royal Academy, and eventually a Knight of the Realm. *Spring*—with the artist's characteristic wealth of detail and careful finish—depicts a flower-bedecked procession of rosy-cheeked children, musicians, and elegant women moving through a Victorian fantasy of ancient Rome. This celebration of spring reflects traditional May Day festivities in England, which were enjoying renewed popularity in the later nineteenth century.

JAMES ENSOR

Belgian, 1860–1949
*Christ's Entry into Brussels
in 1889*, 1888
Oil on canvas
252.5 × 430.5 cm
(99½ × 169½ in.)
87.PA.96

James Ensor's enormous canvas detailing Christ's
entry into the capital city of the artist's native Belgium
presents us with a complex and terrifying vision of the
society of the future. Christ, whose face appears to be
the artist's self-portrait, rides a small donkey in the midst
of a teeming procession of Mardi Gras revelers. Many
in the crowd wear masks, Ensor's device for suggesting
the deceptiveness and artificiality of modern life.

   The canvas's bold color contrasts and thick crusts
of paint give the impression of spontaneity, yet Ensor

planned every figure in advance. In both subject and
technique this masterpiece shocked nineteenth-century
viewers, and it could not be publicly exhibited until
1929. Yet its reputation brought many visitors to the
artist's studio, and its visual and emotional impact
contributed to the development of Expressionism early
in the twentieth century.

Drawings

D rawing is perhaps the most universal, spontaneous, and direct of all
art forms. It embraces a wide variety of techniques, including metalpoint, graphite, pen and ink (often used in conjunction with wash), colored
chalk, and watercolor. It is, moreover, the only art form practiced by most
people, if only at a rudimentary level. The Museum's collection of drawings
was begun in July 1981, five years after the death of J. Paul Getty, when
Rembrandt's red chalk study *Nude Woman with a Snake* was purchased (see
pp. 168 – 69). A year later the Department of Drawings was formed. The
collection now comprises over 600 sheets, including two sketchbooks. The
purpose is to create as representative a collection as possible of the different
schools of Western European drawing from the fourteenth century to the
end of the nineteenth, with emphasis on the work of the most important and
accomplished draftsmen.

    With only a few exceptions, the great artists of the past—painters,
sculptors, printmakers, and architects alike—employed drawing as an inte-
gral part of the creative process. It was used to study nature as well as the
human figure, to explore rough ideas prior to their realization in the more
durable media of paint or stone, and as an end in itself, as in the magnificent
watercolor *Still Life* by Paul Cézanne (see p. 178). Two drawings by the
German Renaissance painter Albrecht Dürer demonstrate contrasting usages
by one artist. His highly finished gouache study of a stag beetle (see
p. 163) was drawn directly from nature and was made as a record in its own
right. The more loosely drawn preparatory *Study of the Good Thief* (see
p. 164) was evidently done for a painting or print representing the Crucifixion,
although no such work has so far been identified. Many of the drawings are
compositional studies for pictures. The *Sheet of Studies for "The Martyrdom
of Saint George"* by the Venetian painter Paolo Veronese (see p. 156), for
example, explores a multitude of solutions. Drawings after the nude model
have always been considered a fundamental step in the training of an artist.
Either as preparatory sketches for larger compositions or as independent
works, they are particularly well represented in this collection. Prud'hon's
Study of a Female Nude (see detail, left, and pp. 172 – 73) is one of the
most spectacular drawings of this type.

    Drawings are sensitive to light and can only be exhibited for short
periods. Those on view at any given time have been brought together
to illustrate some common theme or a particular period in the history of art.

LEONARDO
DA VINCI

Italian, 1452–1519
*Studies for the Christ Child
with a Lamb,* circa 1503–6
Pen and brown ink and
black chalk
21 × 14.2 cm (8¼ × 5⁹⁄₁₆ in.)
86.GG.725

Three of the studies in this drawing are in ink, while
another three are faintly drawn in black chalk. The child
wrestling with the lamb is either the infant Saint John
the Baptist or the Christ Child. The number of different
sketches for the same figural group indicates Leonardo's
painstaking approach to the planning of his compositions. He probably made this drawing in preparation for
a painting of the Virgin and Child with Saint John,
now lost but known through copies. Leonardo inscribed
the drawing at the top of the sheet and on the verso in
his characteristic mirror script.

MICHELANGELO
BUONARROTI

Italian, 1475–1564
*The Holy Family with the
Infant Saint John the Baptist
(The Rest on the Flight into
Egypt)*, circa 1530
Black and red chalk with pen
and brown ink over stylus
underdrawing
28 × 39.4 cm (11 × 15½ in.)
93.GB.51

Michelangelo treated the subject of the Madonna and
Child many times during his long career—in painting
and sculpture, as well as in drawing. Here he chose
to represent an unusual variant of the theme, not specifically related in the Bible, in which the infant Baptist and
two angels join the Holy Family on an interlude in their
flight into Egypt to escape Herod's persecution; on the
right, the ass grazes contentedly, the packsaddle still on
its back.

The drawing's purpose is unknown, although it
may have been made for a low relief. From its style it
may be dated around 1530, during the artist's third
Florentine period (1516–34). Michelangelo studied the
same composition in a number of other sketches, while
a sculpture of the seated Virgin suckling the Christ
Child, in the Medici Chapel, Florence, shares a number
of analogies with the two figures in this drawing.

RAPHAEL

(Raffaello Sanzio)
Italian, 1483–1520
*Saint Paul Rending His
Garments*, circa 1515–16
Metalpoint with white
gouache heightening on pale
violet-gray prepared paper
23 × 10.3 cm (9¹⁄₁₆ × 4¹⁄₁₆ in.)
84.GG.919

This study by Raphael
was made in preparation
for the figure of Saint
Paul in *The Sacrifice of
Lystra*, one of a series of
tapestries commissioned
to decorate the walls
of the Sistine Chapel in
the Vatican. The violent
twisting of the saint's
body is convincingly
rendered by the high-
lighted drapery folds
that accentuate his
movement. Here Raphael
not only elucidates the
pose but gives an insight
into the saint's emotional
state.

LORENZO LOTTO

Italian, circa 1480 – after 1556
*Saint Martin Dividing
His Cloak with a Beggar,*
circa 1530
Brush and gray-brown
wash with white and cream
gouache heightening and
black chalk on brown paper
31.4 × 21.7 cm (12⅜ × 8⁹⁄₁₆ in.)
83.GG.262

The steep perspective suggests that the composition
was intended either for a painted organ shutter or
a fresco to be seen above eye level. The lively movement of the figures and the rich architectural back-
drop anticipate the compositions of the later Baroque
period, although the combination of media is typical
of sixteenth-century Venetian drawing.

PAOLO VERONESE

Italian, 1528–1588
Sheet of Studies for "The Martyrdom of Saint George," 1566
Pen and brown ink and brown wash
28.9 × 21.7 cm (11⅜ × 8⁹⁄₁₆ in.)
83.GA.258

These freely drawn studies are for various sections of Veronese's altarpiece of *The Martyrdom of Saint George* in the church of San Giorgio, Verona. The rapid pen strokes of the sketches reflect the artist's creative energy as he explored varying solutions to the different figural problems posed by the composition. With great sensitivity he subtly altered the media of the studies; some are done in pen and wash, others in pen alone. Although the individual sketches are distinct in character, they are unified by the overall rhythmic flow of the artist's hand as it moved quickly across the page.

ANNIBALE CARRACCI

Italian, 1560–1609
Four Studies of Heads Drawn over a Copy of a "Saint John the Evangelist" by Correggio, circa 1585
Black chalk
27.7 × 20.7 cm (10⅞ × 8⅛ in.)
85.GB.218

Annibale Carracci's style of drawing is admired for its forcefulness. A certain informality in his character made him fond of representing subjects from everyday life. In this sheet he has drawn a bearded man wearing a hat seen in right profile (the two studies top left), a youth with his head cupped in his hands, seen full face (top right), and a youth wearing a hat and gazing downward (bottom of the sheet, with it turned clockwise ninety degrees). This is the sort of drawing that Carracci would have made in his leisure, perhaps while observing his friends or family during a period of relaxation. The sketches are done over an incised drawing after a figure group by Correggio.

FEDERICO ZUCCARO

Italian, circa 1541–1609
*Taddeo Decorating the
Façade of the Palazzo Mattei*,
circa 1590
Pen and brown ink and
brown wash over black chalk
with touches of red chalk
25 × 42.2 cm (9⅞ × 16⅝ in.)
99.GA.6.19

During the 1590s Federico Zuccaro made a series of
twenty drawings depicting the early life of his older
brother and teacher, Taddeo (1529–1566), who is
ranked among the greatest Italian Mannerist artists of
all time. These drawings, all in the Museum's collection,
are a moving tribute, tracing Taddeo's hardships as a
young artist in Rome to his first artistic triumph at age
eighteen. The series culminates with this triumphant
scene showing Taddeo decorating the now destroyed
façade of the Palazzo Mattei with scenes from the life of
the Roman hero Furius Camillus. As young Taddeo
paints on the scaffold, the Three Graces with Spirit and
Pride stand around him, while allegories of Fame fly
above. Marveling at his work are the greatest painters
of Rome: Michelangelo on his horse to the left, with
his servant Urbino, as well as Girolamo Siciolante and
Daniele da Volterra. To the right is the famed artist-
biographer, Giorgio Vasari, shown discussing the façade
with Francesco Salviati.

GIANLORENZO BERNINI

Italian, 1598–1680
*Design for a Fountain, with
a Marine God Clutching a
Dolphin*, circa 1651–52
Black chalk
34.9 × 23.8 cm (13¹¹⁄₁₆ × 9⅜ in.)
87.GB.142

Bernini was an architect and a painter as well as the
most successful Italian sculptor of his day. The subject
of this drawing corresponds with a fountain that he
designed for the central niche of the palace of Duke
Francesco I d'Este at Sassuolo. The liveliness of
the figure as it struggles with the dolphin is typical of
Bernini's vigorous High Baroque style.

GIOVANNI
BATTISTA
PIAZZETTA

Italian, 1683–1754
*A Boy Holding a Pear
(Giacomo Piazzetta?)*,
circa 1737
Black and white chalk on
blue-gray paper (two
joined sheets)
39.2 × 30.9 cm
(15⁷⁄₁₆ × 12¹⁄₁₆ in.)
86.GB.677

Here Piazzetta has drawn a youngster, beautifully dressed in a brocade vest, full-sleeved shirt, and feathered cap. The boy holds up a pear as he gazes meaningfully at the viewer. This same sitter, recognizable from his good-natured demeanor, appears in a number of Piazzetta's other works and has been tentatively identified as the artist's son, Giacomo. The drawing seems to have been made to be enjoyed in its own right, without any ulterior purpose. Piazzetta applied the chalk with varying degrees of pressure. In some areas it is lightly shaded and as a result seems soft and diffused. Elsewhere it is applied more heavily in rich, velvety patches. Piazzetta further enlivened the sheet with white chalk highlights—in the lace collar and linen sleeves, in the pear, and on the tip of the boy's nose.

GIOVANNI
BATTISTA
PIRANESI

Italian, 1720–1778
An Ancient Port,
circa 1749–50
Red and black chalk, brush
and brown and reddish
wash; squared in black chalk
38.5 × 52.8 cm
(15⅛ × 20¹³⁄₁₆ in.)
88.GB.18

Piranesi was one of the greatest etchers in Europe
during the eighteenth century. His best-known prints
are his views of Rome and his architectural fantasies.
This drawing of an ancient port served as a preparatory
study for an etching entitled *Part of a Large Magnificent
Port* that was first published in 1750 in a series entitled
Opere varie. The composition is made up of huge interlocking architectural forms, including a portal and
bridge in the foreground, a triumphal arch in the center,
and a coliseum-like structure, truncated pyramid, and
obelisk in the distance. Each section of this building
complex is decorated with an elaborate sculptural program, and the whole is further dramatized by clouds
of smoke. In the foreground are boats reminiscent of
those found in Piranesi's native Venice.

Piranesi first drew the main outlines in chalk,
then liberally added brown and red wash for shading
and some of the details. The black chalk grid lines
throughout were made to assist the process of transfer-
ring the design to the copperplate. The wash gives
a vibrancy to the whole that was not transmitted to the
etching. Piranesi made at least two drawings preparatory to this finished sketch.

MARTIN
SCHONGAUER

German, 1450/53–1491
Studies of Peonies,
circa 1472/73
Gouache and watercolor
25.7 × 33 cm (10⅛ × 13 in.)
92.GC.80

The flowers (*Paeonia officinalis L.*) were evidently drawn from life. On the left is a stem with one blossom fully open, the head turned away, and one bud; on the right, a separate study of an open blossom, seen from the front. The blossoms and foliage are delicately modeled and colored. This large sheet, the only surviving nature study by Schongauer, is a singularly important drawing in the German Renaissance period. It was used as the model for some of the flowers in the background of his great altarpiece, *The Madonna of the Rose Garden,* painted in 1473 for the Dominican church at Colmar. The drawing is among the earliest manifestations of the urge toward the realistic depiction of nature in Northern Renaissance art and, as such, constitutes a cructial precedent for Albrecht Dürer's nature studies of the early sixteenth century, for example the *Stag Beetle* (see p. 163).

ALBRECHT DÜRER

German, 1471–1528
Stag Beetle, 1505
Watercolor and gouache;
top left corner added; tip
of left antenna painted in by
a later hand
14.2 × 11.4 cm (5⁹⁄₁₆ × 4½ in.)
83.GC.214

This startling image is typical of Dürer's many studies drawn directly from nature. His drawings of this type form an illuminating counterpart to the more obviously scientific renderings of plant and animal life by his Italian near-contemporary Leonardo da Vinci. In this drawing Dürer presents a living creature illusionistically; the beetle casts its own shadow on the plain ground of the paper as if it were actually crawling across it. The modulations of tone along the creature's ridged wing cases are also faithfully rendered.

ALBRECHT DÜRER

German, 1471–1528
Study of the Good Thief,
circa 1505
Pen and brown ink
26.8 × 12.6 cm (10⁹⁄₁₆ × 5 in.)
83.GA.360

In this drawing the figure of the Good Thief is sharply foreshortened, heightening its dramatic impact. The fingers on his right hand are curled in agony, underscoring the emotive force of the whole. In addition, Dürer drew the cross appearing to bend under the man's weight. The use of the pen is completely assured, from the confident handling of the contours of the body to the clear definition and modeling of its forms.

ALBRECHT
ALTDORFER

German, circa 1482/85–1538
Christ Carrying the Cross,
circa 1510–15
Pen and black ink, gray
wash, and black chalk
DIAM: 30.4 cm (11¹⁵⁄₁₆ in.)
86.GG.465

Albrecht Altdorfer was the leading painter of the Danube school. This drawing shows Christ fallen under the weight of the cross, submitting to the blows of his tormentors. Bravura penwork heightens the emotional resonance of the scene. Altdorfer drew the figure of Christ slightly from behind, a viewpoint that has the effect of creating greater space within the composition than a simple profile view. The monumentality of the conception is more consistent with a large-scale painting, although Altdorfer made this drawing as a design for a stained glass window. It is the only such drawing by him known.

HANS BALDUNG GRIEN

German, circa 1484/85–1545
Saint Vincent Ferrer
Preaching the Sermon of the
Last Judgment, circa 1505
Pen and brown ink over slight
black chalk underdrawing
30.8 × 22.3 cm (12⅛ × 8¹¹⁄₁₆ in.)
83.GA.194

This drawing was made as a preparatory study for a stained glass window, a
type of commission Baldung is known
to have undertaken. The presence of
Christ, who is shown in a miniature
apparition above the preacher's left hand,
indicates that the subject is either the
Salvation or the Last Judgment, a
sermon for which Saint Vincent was
famous. Baldung was one of the most
distinguished of Dürer's followers,
and his characteristically rhythmic and
sharply accented pen strokes owe much
to his master's style.

URS GRAF

Swiss, circa 1485–1527/29
Dancing Peasant Couple, 1525
Pen and black ink
20.6 × 14.7 cm (8⅛ × 5¹¹⁄₁₆ in.)
92.GA.72

The graphic work of Urs Graf, who was
a mercenary soldier as well as an artist,
provides a glimpse of the violent and
bawdy aspects of life in early sixteenth-
century Switzerland. This is one of a
series of drawings of peasant dancers
that Graf made either as models for
prints or as independent works of art. In
this drawing a tattered peasant couple
dance with abandon. The man lewdly
grasps his partner's buttock, the meaning
of his gesture reinforced by the phallic
symbolism of the ax and dagger at his
waist. Graf's forceful line work comple-
ments the rawness of his subject matter.

HANS HOLBEIN
THE YOUNGER

Swiss, 1497–1543
Portrait of a Scholar or Cleric,
circa 1532–43
Black and red chalk, pen and
brush and black ink, on pink
prepared paper
21.9 × 18.5 cm (8⅝ × 7¼ in.)
84.GG.93

Because of his hat, the unidentified sitter is taken to be
either a cleric or a scholar. Holbein probably made the
portrait during his second English period (1532–43),
when he served as painter to King Henry VIII, and the
sitter may well have been connected with the Tudor
court. Holbein sketched the contours of the man's face
in black chalk and then deftly went over them in black
ink. The face was softly modeled in red chalk, using the
pink of the paper as a middle tone. Outside the face,
the handling is broad and painterly, as in the hair and
robe. Holbein was attuned to the uniqueness of the
features of each of his sitters, which he rendered with
unparalleled precision and objectivity. For this reason
his portrait drawings present sixteenth-century per-
sonalities with greater freshness and fullness than the
works of almost any other artist of his time.

PIETER JANSZ.
SAENREDAM

Dutch, 1597–1665
The Choir and North Ambula-
tory of the Church of Saint
Bavo, Haarlem, 1634
Red chalk, graphite, pen and
brown ink, and watercolor,
the outlines indented for
transfer (recto); rubbed with
black chalk for transfer
(verso)
37.7 × 39.3 cm
(14¹³⁄₁₆ × 15⁷⁄₁₆ in.)
88.GC.131

Saenredam specialized in painting architectural subjects. Between 1634 and 1636 he made a number of
drawings and paintings of the church of Saint Bavo in
Haarlem, one of Holland's largest and most venerated
Gothic buildings. This elaborate watercolor drawing,
which is dated November 1634, is based on a sketch
the artist drew on the spot in October 1634, now in the
Gemeentearchief, Haarlem. The Museum's drawing is
a finished preparatory study, with some differences in
the proportions of the design, for the painting on panel
now in the Muzeum Naradowe, Warsaw. The outlines
of the drawing were traced directly onto the panel.
An inscription on the Museum's drawing states that the
painting was completed on October 15, 1635.

REMBRANDT
HARMENSZ.
VAN RIJN

Dutch, 1606–1669
*Landscape with the House
with the Little Tower,*
circa 1651–52
Pen and brown ink and
brown wash
9.7 × 21.5 cm (3 ¹³/₁₆ × 8 ⁷/₁₆ in.)
83.GA.363

This is among the most sensitive and abstract of
Rembrandt's landscape drawings. Space and atmosphere
in the foreground are suggested by only a few lines,
while a complex mixture of thinner lines, dots, and
touches of wash creates a richer and more varied background. The drawing illustrates how a great artist can
evoke vast space with a supreme economy of means.

REMBRANDT
HARMENSZ.
VAN RIJN

Dutch, 1606–1669
Nude Woman with a Snake,
circa 1637
Red chalk with white
gouache heightening
24.7 × 13.7 cm (9 ¹¹/₁₆ × 5 ⁷/₁₆ in.)
81.GB.27

This is one of the best preserved and most fluent of all
of Rembrandt's red chalk drawings. The figure, which
is probably intended to represent Eve, is here shown
as an ordinary woman and not as an idealized type.
She presents her bare breast to the spectator and grips
the neck of a large snake that coils around her leg.
The range of draftsmanship is striking, from the fine
modeling of the figure to the virtuoso passages of
freely sketched drapery.

PETER PAUL
RUBENS

Flemish, 1577–1640
Korean Man, circa 1617–18
Black and red chalk
38.4 × 23.5 cm (15⅛ × 9¼ in.)
83.GB.384

Rubens used this imposing portrait of a man in formal costume as the basis for one of the background figures in his painting *The Miracles of Saint Francis Xavier*. The subject's woven horsehair hat identifies him as Korean, and he appears to be among the earliest representations of a Korean visitor to Europe. It is one of Rubens's most finely executed drawn portraits, with the likeness enlivened by the touches of red in the face. The meticulous detailing of the flesh contrasts with the much broader rendering of the voluminous robe.

NICOLAS POUSSIN

French, 1594 – 1665
*Apollo and the Muses
on Mount Parnassus,*
circa 1626/27 or 1631/32
Pen and brown ink and
brown wash
17.6 × 24.5 cm (6¹⁵⁄₁₆ × 9¹¹⁄₁₆ in.)
83.GG.345

Poussin was an admirer of Raphael as well as of the
ancient classical tradition. The composition of this
drawing was inspired by Raphael's famous fresco in the
Stanza della Segnatura in the Vatican. The handling,
with broad washes, is unusually animated for Poussin.
Nevertheless, the artist shows his characteristic ten-
dency toward abstraction of form. The drawing
is a first idea for a painting now in the Prado, Madrid.

JEAN-ANTOINE WATTEAU

French, 1684 – 1721
*Two Studies of a Flutist and
One of the Head of a Boy,*
circa 1716 – 17
Red, black, and white chalk
21.4 × 33.6 cm (8⁷⁄₁₆ × 13¹⁄₁₆ in.)
88.GB.3

Watteau was one of the most influential artists and
gifted draftsmen of the French Rococo period. A master
of lyrical themes, he invented the subject known as the
fête galante, in which elegant young men and women
in an open landscape dally to the sound of music, capti-
vated by feelings of love. Watteau probably made
this drawing while attending a concert. He studied the
flute player from different angles, recording distinct
expressions on the musician's face. The boy at the left
appears to be listening. Watteau was a master of the
technique known as *trois crayons*, a combination of red,
black, and white chalk, almost invariably drawn on
tinted paper.

JEAN-AUGUSTE-DOMINIQUE INGRES

French, 1780–1867
*Portrait of Lord
Grantham*, 1816
Graphite
40.5 × 28.2 cm
(15¹⁵⁄₁₆ × 11⅛ in.)
82.GD.106

This drawing of Thomas Philip Robinson, third Baron
Grantham and later Earl de Grey, is signed and dated
1816. Ingres had a lucrative practice as a portrait drafts-
man while he lived in Italy, from 1806 to 1824. Many of
his patrons were foreign residents or wealthy travelers
on their Grand Tours. The drawn portraits of Ingres are
renowned for their severity of line, which exemplifies
his strongly classical style.

PIERRE-PAUL PRUD'HON

French, 1758–1823
Study of a Female Nude,
circa 1800
Black and white chalk,
stumped, on blue paper
60.4 × 31.8 cm (23¾ × 12½ in.)
99.GB.49

Prud'hon was celebrated for his series of exquisite chalk
drawings known as *académies*, or studies of nude models posed in the studio. Made as an independent work
of art, the present example is one of his most superb
portrayals of the female nude. Her classically inspired
pose, combined with the shimmering white surface of
her skin, is evocative of antique marble sculpture. Far
from statuary, however, Prud'hon's figure seemingly
trembles before our eyes through a blend of infinite tiny
strokes of white chalk and smoky passages of stumped
black chalk. Her dreamy gaze and the soft play of
shadows across her flesh add to the inherent aura of
sensuality.

EUGÈNE
DELACROIX

French, 1798–1863
The Education of Achilles,
circa 1860–62
Pastel
30.6 × 41.9 cm (12¹/₁₆ × 16½ in.)
86.GG.728

Delacroix was a leading painter of the Romantic movement in France. He greatly admired the work of Peter
Paul Rubens, and his own paintings reflect this influence in their free handling and bright colors. Delacroix
often represented exotic themes, especially those of
the Orient.

The subject of this pastel, taken from Greek mythology, is Achilles learning the art of hunting from
the Centaur Chiron. The energy of the figures as they
gallop through the landscape is matched by Delacroix's
own vigorous touch. The palette is characteristically
rich, consisting of dark greens, blues, and browns, which
are varied by light flesh tones and reds. Delacroix
completed two paintings of the same composition. He
made this pastel as a gift for his friend the writer
George Sand, who had expressed her admiration for
those paintings.

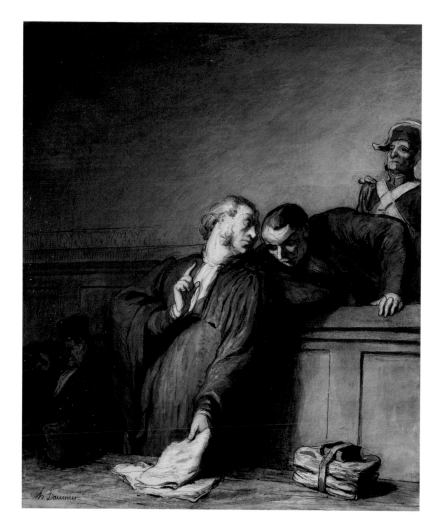

HONORÉ DAUMIER

French, 1808–1879
A Criminal Case, circa 1860
Watercolor and gouache
with pen and brown ink and
black chalk
38.5 × 32.8 cm
(15⅛ × 12¹³⁄₁₆ in.)
89.GA.33

Best known for his satirical lithographs, Daumier also
made drawings, watercolors, paintings, and sculptures.
This watercolor is datable to the later part of his career,
when his style had become broader and his paintings
more monumental in effect. It shows a courtroom scene,
with an attorney looking back to his client, and is
characteristic of Daumier's incisive depictions of judges,
lawyers, and criminals.

GUSTAVE
COURBET

French, 1828–1875
*Sleeping Bacchante
(Jeanne Zélie-Mélodie
Courbet)*, 1847
Charcoal
50.3 × 38 cm
(19¾ × 15¼ in.)
99.GE.43

Pioneer of the Realist movement, Courbet elevated the subject of common humanity to the level of monumental, timeless grandeur. Courbet's magnificent portrait of his sister Zélie is one of the few large-scale, signed, and finished drawings he made as pictures. The smudged, painterly application of charcoal suggests the heaviness of Zélie's slumber. White paper, in reserve, glows with the translucence of youthful flesh. The girl's costume raises uncertainties. Has she whimsically placed the grape leaves in her hair, or does Courbet intend to portray her as an ancient bacchante, worshiper of Bacchus, god of wine? Does Zélie dream of that classical past? Such provocative combinations of the past and the present led Courbet to declare Realism "a living art."

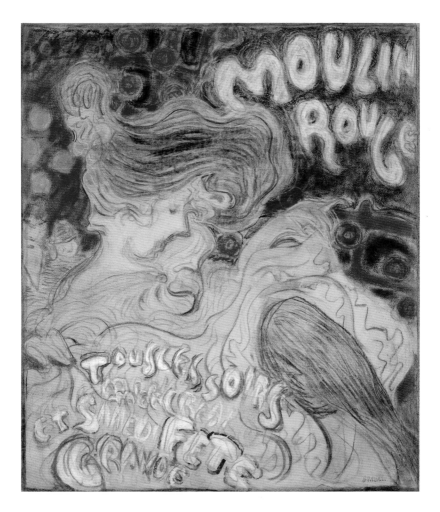

PIERRE BONNARD

French, 1867–1947
The Moulin Rouge, 1891
Pastel and charcoal
54.7 × 48.3 cm
(21½ × 19 1/16 in.)
99.GG.32

The colorful sights that enlivened Parisian nightclubs, theaters, and circuses during the 1890s inspired the young Bonnard, a principal member of Paris's avant-garde artistic community. This is a highly worked model for Bonnard's second poster project advertising the legendary nightclub in Montmartre, the Moulin Rouge. A young dancer wearing a large, undulating hat lifts her frothy underskirts. With her stockinged leg raised to the height of her shoulders, she performs the famous can-can, the high-kick dance synonymous with Paris's renowned nightlife. Her delicate profile, hair, and hands are outlined in neon-yellow pastel, evoking the glow of stage lights. The dynamically fluid lines sweep the pictorial elements together into a giddying spin of forms, letters, and colors. The background pulsates with expressive color and movement: the jarring reds and purple evoke the bawdy nocturnal atmosphere of the Moulin Rouge in Paris's Montmartre district.

PAUL CÉZANNE

French, 1839 – 1906
Still Life, circa 1900
Watercolor over graphite
48 × 63.1 cm (18¹⁵⁄₁₆ × 24⅞ in.)
83.GC.221

This is one of the largest and most finished of Cézanne's watercolors. In its complexity it shares many of the qualities of his paintings. The technique of superimposed layers of translucent watercolor suggests the plasticity of forms with extraordinary resonance, in spite of the frailty of the medium. The contrast between the colored washes and the untouched passages of white paper enhances the monumental effect.

VINCENT
VAN GOGH

Dutch, 1853–1890
Portrait of Joseph Roulin, 1888
Reed and quill pens and
brown ink and black chalk
32 × 24.4 cm (12⅝ × 9⅝ in.)
85.GA.299

Joseph Roulin was a postal worker with whom Van Gogh
became friends during his stay in Arles from 1888 to
1889. Roulin and his wife and children sat for Van Gogh
many times. The artist wrote that the postman's physical
appearance and philosophy reminded him of Socrates;
he was "neither embittered, nor happy, nor always
irreproachably just." Van Gogh's strong impression of
Roulin is evident in the sitter's close-up, frontal pose
and intense gaze. The drawing is animated by the patterns of his clothing and beard, drawn with two different pens and various techniques of hatching, shading,
and stippling to achieve the remarkable range of textures.

FRANCISCO JOSÉ DE
GOYA Y LUCIENTES

Spanish, 1746–1828
Contemptuous of the Insults,
circa 1808–12
Brush and india ink
29.5 × 18.2 cm (11⅝ × 7³⁄₁₆ in.)
82.GG.96

This sheet was once part of an album of drawings that
Goya seems to have made for his private use. Drawn
with great tonal subtlety and fluidity, it shows a gentle-
man expressing disdain for the insults of gnomes,
possibly a symbol of Goya's contempt for the soldiers
who caused great devastation in Spain during the
Napoleonic Wars (1803–15).

WILLIAM BLAKE

British, 1757–1827
Satan Exulting over Eve, 1795
Watercolor, pen and black
ink, and graphite over
color print
42.6 × 53.5 cm (16¾ × 21¹/₁₆ in.)
84.GC.49

Although Blake was one of the greatest British artists
of the Romantic period, he is less well known than
some of his contemporaries. One reason for this is the
poetic and visionary basis of his art, which embodies
his own personal philosophy and mythology. His powerful images reflect his visions, which he insists were
not "a cloudy vapour or a nothing; they are organized
and minutely articulated beyond all that the mortal
and perishing nature can produce." Yet, in spite of this
subjective inspiration, the compositional formulae
and figure types in his work depend on those of the great
old master tradition of painting and drawing, works
with which he was familiar from engravings.

Satan Exulting over Eve belongs to the gray area
between drawing and printmaking. It is one of twelve
color prints Blake created in 1795 by drawing and
brushing a design in broad color areas on a piece of
millboard, printing them on a piece of paper, and working them over considerably in watercolor and pen and
ink. Each version of the various designs is therefore
unique. Satan flies in malevolent glory over the beautiful nude figure of Eve, who is entwined by his alter
ego, the serpent of the Garden of Eden.

Blake was trained as an engraver. Most of his career
was spent publishing his own uniquely illustrated poetry
and prose.

Decorative Arts

The Museum's collection of decorative arts—of which approximately twenty percent is illustrated here—consists mainly of objects made in Paris from the mid-seventeenth to the end of the eighteenth century. It contains furniture, silver, ceramics, tapestries, carpets, and objects made of gilt bronze. The latter includes wall lights, chandeliers, firedogs, and clocks. All of these objects are displayed in chronological order in fifteen galleries, four of which are fitted with eighteenth-century paneling.

J. Paul Getty began to purchase European furniture in the late 1930s and continued to acquire slowly until the 1960s. Then, having opened his original small museum in Malibu, he stopped collecting for a time. At this point the entire collection of decorative arts consisted of about thirty objects and was housed in two galleries.

With the prospect of filling the much larger museum that was to open in 1974, Getty began to acquire again in the early 1970s and continued to do so until his death in 1976. In this period strong roots were put down, and some new curatorial policies were established. Gradually, a conception began to be realized, that of forming a representative collection of French decorative arts from the early years of the reign of Louis XIV (1643–1715) to the end of the reign of Louis XVI (1774–1792).

With the formation of the J. Paul Getty Trust, the confines of the collection were expanded to include objects made in other European countries, primarily Germany and Italy. Growth and expansion have been gradual; only the finest pieces were acquired, gleaned from an international market sometimes restricted by laws pertaining to legal exportation. In this Museum, set in the hills of the Santa Monica Mountains, the collection is comfortably displayed, allowing a number of pieces formerly kept in storage to be viewed at last.

ONE OF A SET OF TEN PANELS

Design attributed to Charles Le Brun (*premier peintre du Roi* 1664; 1619 – 1690)
French (Paris), circa 1650 – 60
Painted and gilded oak
Illustration (.4):
202.8 × 69.7 cm
(6 ft. 11⅛ in. × 2 ft. 3⅞ in.)
91.DH.18.1 – 10

These panels form part of an ensemble that would have been used to line a room in a château or a grand *hôtel* in Paris. Two are painted with an as-yet unidentified monogram, and traces of a Maltese cross can be seen on some of them. One of the smaller panels exactly resembles in its design a painted panel still in situ in the *bibliothèque* (library) of the Château de Vaux-le-Vicomte. That painted room was made for the finance minister Nicolas Fouquet by Charles Le Brun in 1659. The florid, highly colored design is typical of Le Brun's style. Many of the elements of the design reappear in his later works made for Louis XIV, especially the series of large Savonnerie carpets.

READING AND WRITING TABLE

French (Paris), circa 1670–75
Walnut and oak veneered
with ivory, blue-painted horn,
rosewood, and amaranth;
gilt-bronze moldings; steel;
modern silk velvet
63.5 × 48.5 × 35.5 cm
(2 ft. 1 in. × 1 ft. 7⅛ in.
× 1 ft. 2 in.)
83.DA.21

This small table, described in a posthumous inventory of Louis XIV, is one of the few surviving pieces of furniture to have belonged to that great monarch. Among the rarest and earliest pieces in the collection, it is decorated with ivory and horn that has been painted blue underneath, perhaps to resemble lapis lazuli. The table is fitted with an adjustable writing surface and a drawer constructed to contain writing equipment.

TABLE

Attributed to Pierre
Golle (circa 1620–1684,
master before 1656)
French (Paris), circa 1680
Oak veneered with brass,
pewter, tortoiseshell, and
ebony, with ebony drawers;
gilded fruitwood and gilt-
bronze mounts
76.7 × 42 × 36.1 cm
(2 ft. 6½ in. × 1 ft. 4½ in.
× 1 ft. 2¼ in.)
82.DA.34

The top of this small table unfolds to
reveal a scene of three women taking tea
beneath a canopy. It is therefore likely
that the table was intended to support a
tea tray. The table is decorated with four
large dolphins and four fleurs-de-lis,
all in tortoiseshell. These emblems were
used by the Grand Dauphin, son of
Louis XIV, for whom this table and its
pair, now in the British Royal Collection, probably were made. The scene
on the top was copied after a drawing
by the Huguenot ornamentalist and
engraver Daniel Marot, which was later
engraved in the early eighteenth century.

CABINET ON STAND

Attributed to André-Charles
Boulle (1642–1732, master
before 1666)
French (Paris), circa 1675–80
Oak veneered with pewter,
brass, tortoiseshell, horn,
ebony, ivory, and wood
marquetry; bronze mounts;
painted, gilded figures; with
drawers of snakewood
229.9 × 151.2 × 66.7 cm
(7 ft. 6½ in. × 4 ft. 11½ in.
× 2 ft. 2¼ in.)
77.DA.1

This cabinet was probably made by André-Charles
Boulle for Louis XIV, whose likeness appears in a
bronze medallion above the central door, or as a royal
gift. The medallion is flanked by military trophies,
while the marquetry on the door below shows the
cockerel of France triumphant over the eagle of
the Holy Roman Empire and the lion of Spain and the
Spanish Netherlands. The cabinet is supported by two
large figures, the one on the right being Hercules.
Clearly made to glorify Louis XIV's victories, this piece
is one of a pair; the other is privately owned.

TABLE

Attributed to André-Charles
Boulle (1642 – 1732, master
before 1666)
French (Paris), circa 1680
Oak veneered with brass,
pewter, tortoiseshell, ebony,
horn, ivory, and marquetry
of stained and natural
woods; gilt-bronze mounts
72 × 110.5 × 73.6 cm
(2 ft. 4⅛ in. × 3 ft. 7½ in.
× 2 ft. 5 in.)
71.DA.100

This table is among the few pieces of furniture veneered
with both wood and tortoiseshell, and brass and pewter that survive from the late seventeenth century.
Based upon the combination of these materials and the
fine craftsmanship, it is attributed to André-Charles
Boulle. The naturalistic marquetry flowers that enrich
its top, sides, and stretcher are recognizable: peonies,
hyacinths, daffodils, tulips, and ranunculus, among
others. Inventory documents record the presence of
similar tables in the residences of Louis XIV, although
this example cannot be precisely identified.

One of Two Coffers on Stands

Attributed to André-Charles Boulle (1642–1732, master before 1666)
French (Paris), circa 1684–89
Oak, cypress, and walnut veneered with tortoiseshell, blue-painted horn, ebony, rosewood, pewter, and brass; gilt-bronze mounts; mirror glass
156.6 × 89.9 × 55.8 cm
(5 ft. 1⅝ in. × 2 ft. 11⅜ in. × 1 ft. 10 in.)
82.DA.109.1–.2

This coffer and its pendant were almost certainly made by André-Charles Boulle at a time when he was making numerous pieces of furniture for the Grand Dauphin, son of Louis XIV. A coffer of similar form delivered by Boulle is listed in the Grand Dauphin's inventory of 1689. Such coffers were intended to hold jewelry and other precious objects. The large gilt-bronze straps at the front and sides can be let down to reveal small drawers.

ONE OF A SET OF
SEVEN TAPESTRIES

Woven under the direction
of Philippe Béhagle
(active 1684–1705)
French,
Beauvais manufactory,
circa 1697–1705
Wool and silk;
modern cotton lining
424 × 319 cm
(13 ft. 11 in. × 10 ft. 5½ in.)
83.DD.338

The Astronomers is one of a set of tapestries from the
series entitled The Story of the Emperor of China.
It shows Emperor Shun Chih (1644–1661) in conver-
sation with members of his court and the European
Jesuit Father Adam Schall von Bell (1592–1666) around
a large globe. This was the first French tapestry series
to be created around a chinoiserie theme; it established
a long-lasting taste for the exotic and contributed to
the success of the Beauvais manufactory. The set,
originally consisting of ten hangings, was woven for
Louis-Alexandre, comte de Toulouse (1678–1737),
the second legitimized son of Louis XIV. The border
bears his coat of arms and monogram.

DESK

French (Paris), circa 1700
Oak, fir, cherry, beech, and
walnut; veneered with brass,
tortoiseshell, mother-of-pearl,
pewter, copper, ebony, and
painted and unpainted horn;
with silvered and gilt-bronze
mounts
70.5 × 89 × 51 cm
(2 ft. 3¼ in. ×
2 ft. 11 in. × 1 ft. 8 in.)
87.DA.77

The top of this small desk bears an unidentified coat of
arms (a later replacement) beneath an electoral crown,
surrounded by the Collar and the Order of the Toison
d'Or and supported by standing, crowned lions. The
original pierced steel key for the desk drawers bears the
interlaced monogram ME beneath the electoral crown,
confirming that the desk was made for Maximilian II
Emanuel, Elector of Bavaria (1662–1726). In a partial
inventory of Maximilian's possessions taken in Munich
in 1704, a number of pieces of furniture are briefly
described as being veneered with brass, pewter, and
tortoiseshell. He obviously had a liking for highly
decorated furniture, such as this small desk, which was
made for him in Paris.

Ewer

Ewer: Chinese, Kangxi
(1662 – 1722)
Mounts: French (Paris),
circa 1700 – 10
Hard-paste porcelain, polychrome enamel decoration;
gilt-bronze mounts
46.1 × 35.2 × 13.8 cm
(1 ft. 6⅛ in. × 1 ft. 1⅞ in.
× 5⅜ in.)
82.DI.3

This ewer is an early example of
the Parisian fashion for fitting Oriental
porcelain with gilt-bronze mounts.
Throughout the late seventeenth and
eighteenth centuries the French had
a passion for objects from the Far East
but were not content with the original
simple lines and elegant proportions.
They preferred to add gilt-bronze
or silver mounts, in keeping with the
luxurious tastes of the nobility.

MEDAL CABINET

Attributed to André-Charles
Boulle (1642–1732, master
before 1666)
French (Paris), circa 1710–15
Oak and fir veneered with
ebony, brass, amaranth, kingwood, and tortoiseshell; gilt-
bronze mounts; *sarrancolin
des Pyrénées* marble top
82.5 × 140 × 72.5 cm
(2 ft. 8½ in. × 4 ft. 7¼ in.
× 2 ft. 4½ in.)
84.DA.58

The pair to this cabinet, in the State Hermitage, Saint
Petersburg, retains its twenty-four shallow drawers
for medals. These cabinets are of unique form and obviously were commissioned by a wealthy collector of
ancient coins or medals. A pair of cabinets of similar
form is listed in an inventory taken at the death of
Jules-Robert de Cotte in 1767. It is possible that he had
inherited the cabinets from his illustrious father, the
royal architect Robert de Cotte. The latter was closely
associated with André-Charles Boulle, whose style the
cabinets represent well.

MODEL FOR A MANTEL CLOCK

French (Paris), circa 1700
Terracotta; enameled metal
plaques
78.7 × 52.1 × 24.2 cm
(2 ft. 7 in. × 1 ft. 8½ in.
× 9½ in.)
72.DB.52

It is remarkable that this full-size terracotta model for a
clock has survived in such a good state of preservation.
It was often the custom in the eighteenth century for
a model to be ordered from a cabinetmaker for approval
before the finished object was made. All of the very
few such models that survive today date from the late
eighteenth century. No clock of this model, which features the Rape of Persephone by Pluto below the dial,
seems to exist. It is possible that the model was made by
one of the royal craftsmen, such as André-Charles
Boulle, for the approval of Louis XIV.

TAPESTRY

Woven under the direction
of Jean de la Croix (active
1662 – 1712)
French, Gobelins manu-
factory, before 1712
Wool and silk; modern cotton
interface and linen lining
317.5 × 330.8 cm
(10 ft. 5 in. × 10 ft. 10¼ in.)
85.DD.309

This tapestry, representing the month of December and
the Château de Monceaux, is one of a series of twelve,
emblematic of the months of the year and of French
royal splendor. Each weaving portrays Louis XIV in a
daily activity, a royal residence, and a selection of the
monarch's riches and exotic animals. The series was
conceived by Charles Le Brun for production at the
royal workshop at Gobelins, and seven complete sets,
woven with gold thread, were made for the Crown
between 1668 and 1711. This example, however, is one
of a number made as private commissions and bears
the weaver's name.

One of a Pair of Screens

French, Savonnerie
manufactory, circa 1714–40
Wool and linen; cotton twill
gimp; wooden interior
frame and modern velvet
273.6 × 193.2 cm
(8 ft. 11¾ in. × 6 ft. 4⅛ in.)
83.DD.260.1 –.2

This three-paneled screen of knotted wool pile was made
in the Savonnerie workshops, the royal manufactory
that produced carpets, screens, and upholstery covers
exclusively for the French Crown. Jean-Baptiste Belin
de Fontenay (1653 – 1715) and Alexandre-François
Desportes (1661 – 1743) provided the cartoons for this,
one of the two largest models. This example retains its
original brilliant coloring.

CARPET

French (Beauvais or Lille)
or Flemish (Brussels),
circa 1690–1720
Wool and silk
374.3 × 249.5 cm
(12 ft. 3⅜ in. × 8 ft. 2¼ in.)
86.DC.633

The manufactory of this tapestry carpet has not been identified, but its style
and color suggest an origin in northeastern France or in Flanders toward
the end of the seventeenth century. The
floral garlands are reminiscent of borders designed for tapestries produced in
Brussels, while the mustard-yellow
ground color (now faded) is associated
with a popular color known as *tabac
d'Espagne* introduced at the Beauvais
factory around 1685–90. Woven carpets
of this date are extremely rare.

COMMODE

Made by Étienne Doirat
(circa 1675/80–1732)
French (Paris), circa 1725–30
Oak, fir, and walnut
veneered with kingwood
and amaranth; gilt-bronze
mounts; *brèche d'Alep* top
86.4 × 168.9 × 71.7 cm
(2 ft. 10 in. × 5 ft. 6½ in.
× 2 ft. 4¼ in.)
72.DA.66

Doirat, whose name is stamped on this commode, often
worked for the German market. Since the rule requiring
that all works be stamped with the maker's name was
only instituted by the Parisian guild of *menuisiers-
ébénistes* in 1751, it is unusual to find a piece of furniture stamped at this early date.

This commode may well have been intended for
a German patron who would have liked its large scale,
its exaggerated *bombé* shape, and the profusion of
mounts. The lower drawer is provided with a small
wheel, located at the front in the center, to support
its weight and to facilitate its opening.

TERRESTRIAL GLOBE

Painted decoration attributed
to the workshop of Guillaume
and Étienne-Simon Martin
(active 1727–circa 1780)
Terrestrial map engraved
by Louis Borde
(active 1730–1740s)
French (Paris), 1728–30
Printed paper; papier-mâché;
gilt bronze; poplar, spruce,
and alder painted with *vernis
Martin*; bronze; glass
110 × 45 × 32 cm (3 ft. 7 in. ×
1 ft. 5½ in. × 1 ft. ½ in.)
86.DH.705.1–.2

This globe and its accompanying celestial globe were designed and assembled
by Abbé Jean-Antoine Nollet (1700–
1770), a fashionable scientist who taught
physics to the royal children. The terrestrial globe bears a dedication to the
duchesse du Maine, the wife of Louis
XIV's first illegitimate child, and is dated
1728. The celestial globe is dedicated
to her nephew, Louis de Bourbon, comte
de Clermont, and is dated 1730. The
stands are painted with a yellow *vernis*
ground, polychrome flowers, and red
cartouches bearing chinoiserie scenes.
This work probably was carried out
by the Martin brothers, who obtained a
monopoly for their varnish in the mid-
eighteenth century.

Many contemporary portraits show
the sitter with a globe close by, and such
objects came to be considered essential
adornments for the *bibliothèques* and
cabinets of the aristocracy.

SIDE TABLE

French (Paris), circa 1730
Gessoed and gilded oak;
brèche violette top
89.3 × 170.2 × 81.3 cm
(2 ft. 11⅛ in. × 5 ft. 7 in.
× 2 ft. 8 in.)
79.DA.68

This table is intricately carved with lions' heads, drag-
ons, serpents, and chimerae, or composite mythological beasts. While the carving is deep and pierced in
many areas, the table has remarkable strength and is
well able to support its heavy marble top. It was originally part of a set including two smaller side tables;
they would have stood in a large *salon* fitted with paneled
walls carved with similar elements. It is possible that
chairs, a settee, and a fire screen, all similarly carved,
once completed the furnishings of the room.

ONE OF A PAIR
OF ARMCHAIRS

French (Paris), circa 1730–35
Gessoed and gilded beech;
brass casters; modern silk
upholstery
108.5 × 72.3 × 63.4 cm
(3 ft. 6¼ in. × 2 ft. 4½ in.
× 2 ft. 1 in.)
94.DA.10.1 – .2

The design of this armchair dates from
the early years of the Rococo style,
which introduced characteristic elements
such as the scrolling shape of the arm-
rests where they join the seat rail, cabo-
chons surrounded by auricular forms,
and well-defined leaf and plant forms.

TAPESTRY

Woven under the direction
of Étienne-Claude Le Blond
(active 1727–1751)
French, Gobelins manu-
factory, circa 1730–40
Wool and silk; modern
cotton lining
262.7 × 280.6 cm
(11 ft. 10⅛ in. × 9 ft. 2½ in.)
85.DD.100

Tapestries of this form, called *portières*, were used
extensively during the seventeenth and eighteenth centuries in French royal residences, where they were
hung over nearly every door in the grand *appartements*.
They traditionally were decorated with symbols of
royal power. This example, though designed by Pierre-
Josse Perrot (active 1724–1750) for Louis XV (reigned
1715–1774), incorporates symbols—such as the
head of the god Apollo—that were associated with the
king's great-grandfather, Louis XIV, the Sun King.
Twenty-eight *portières* of this model were woven.

Wall Clock

Movement made by
Charles Voisin (1685 – 1761,
master 1710)
French (Paris) and Chantilly
manufactory, circa 1740
Soft-paste porcelain, polychrome enamel decoration;
gilt-bronze mounts;
enameled metal dial; glass
74.9 × 35.6 × 11.1 cm
(2 ft. 5½ in. × 1 ft. 2 in.
× 4⅜ in.)
81.DB.81

The case of this clock was made of soft-paste porcelain
at the Chantilly manufactory, which was established
in 1725 by the prince de Condé. The prince was a great
collector of Japanese porcelain, and initially the Chantilly manufactory produced wares in the Japanese style.
This clock may have been intended to hang over a bed
and is fitted with a repeating mechanism; the pull of
a string makes it strike the time to the nearest hour and
a quarter, enabling the owner to learn the time at night
without having to light a candle.

CONSOLE TABLE

German (Northern?),
circa 1735–45
Gessoed and gilded spruce;
brèche d'Alep top
91.4 × 108.6 × 53.3 cm
(3 ft. × 3 ft. 6¾ in. × 1 ft. 9 in.)
85.DA.319

This console table exhibits the fanciful heights and
extravagant forms achieved by German craftsmen
working during the Rococo period. It is carved entirely
with fantastic motifs intermixed with more traditional
ones. This combination of incongruous elements—
birds, a dragon, hunting implements, lightning bolts,
and fruited vines—appears occasionally in German
expressions of chinoiserie, the Western adaptation and
interpretation of images derived from the Far East.

ONE OF A PAIR OF EWERS

Porcelain: Chinese, Kangxi
reign, 1662–1722
Mounts: French (Paris), 1745–49
Hard-paste porcelain, celadon
ground color, and underglaze
decoration; gilt-bronze mounts
60 × 33 × 21.5 cm
(1 ft. 11⅝ in. × 1 ft. 1 in. × 8½ in.)
78.DI.9.1–.2

These Chinese porcelain vases were
transformed in Paris with the addition
of gilt-bronze mounts into decorative
ewers. This vase shape and the type
of decoration, a celadon ground color
with underglaze decoration, was
first introduced during the reign of the
Chinese emperor Kangxi.

Group of "Japanese" Figures

Modeled by Johann Joachim
Kändler (1706–1775)
German, Meissen manu-
factory, circa 1745
Hard-paste porcelain, polychrome enamel decoration,
and gilding; gilt-bronze
mounts
45.1 × 29.5 × 21.7 cm
(1 ft. 5¾ in. × 11⅝ in. ×
8 9/16 in.)
83.DI.271

This piece is documented to have been modeled by
Kändler, who was among the foremost European ceramic
modelers of the eighteenth century and certainly the
most important modeler at Meissen. An entry in his
workbook for November 20, 1745, clearly describes this
group. This unusually large piece is one of only two
known examples.

The document describes this piece as "a large Japanese Group" (*eine grosse Japanische Grouppee*) even
though the figures appear to be Chinese. This merely
exhibits the confusion that often occurred in Europe
during the eighteenth century regarding the Orient;
the exoticism of the image was more important than a
specific reference. Therefore, this group is typical of
chinoiserie ornamentation (which was a Western adaptation and interpretation of images derived from the
Far East). Indeed, this composition is probably after a
design by a French eighteenth-century painter and may
be from a series representing the five senses.

One of a Pair of Mounted Ceramic Groups

Figure, rockwork, and lion: Chinese, Kangxi (1662–1722); spheres: Chinese, Qianlong, 1736–95; flowers: French, Chantilly manufactory, circa 1740; mounts: French (Paris), circa 1740–45
Hard- and soft-paste porcelain, polychrome enamel decoration; gilt-bronze mounts
30.4 × 22.8 × 12.7 cm
(1 ft. × 9 in. × 5 in.)
78.DI.4.1–.2

As is often the case with eighteenth-century groups of mounted Oriental porcelain, this example is composed of disparate elements never intended to be used together. The boy was made to be freestanding. The rockery originally formed a base for the lion, but these elements were separated and the perfume ball placed in between.

One of a Pair of Decorative Bronzes

Painted decoration attributed to the workshop of Guillaume and Étienne-Simon Martin (active circa 1725–1780)
Bronzes: French (Paris), 1745–49
Silver: French (Paris), 1738–50
Painted bronze; silver
22.8 × 11.5 × 15.2 cm
(9 in. × 4½ in. × 6 in.)
88.DH.127.1–.2

This bronze of a boy carrying a silver bundle of sugar cane and its pair are ornamental figures masquerading as sugar casters that probably were not intended to be functional. They originally belonged to Madame de Pompadour, mistress of Louis XV.

ONE OF A PAIR OF TUREENS AND STANDS

Made by Thomas Germain
(1673 – 1748)
French (Paris), 1744 – 50
Silver
Tureen: 30 × 34.9 × 28.2 cm
(11⁷⁄₁₆ in. × 1 ft. 1¾ in. × 11⅛ in.)
Stand: 4.2 × 46.2 × 47.2 cm
(1⅝ in. × 1 ft. 6³⁄₁₆ in.
× 1 ft. 6⁹⁄₁₆ in.)
82.DG.13.1 – .2

This large tureen and stand, along with its pair, are
marked for the years 1744 to 1750. They are attributed
to the royal silversmith Thomas Germain, who died in
1748, but may have been completed by his son, François-
Thomas Germain. Both father and son were exceptionally skilled craftsmen who served many European royal
courts, especially those of France and Portugal. The
finely worked vegetables and crustaceans on the lid,
probably cast from natural models, demonstrate the
virtuoso talent of the silversmith.

ONE OF A PAIR OF COMMODES

Carving attributed to Joachim
Dietrich (d. 1753)
German (Munich), circa 1745
Painted, gessoed, and gilded
pine; gilt-bronze mounts;
jaune rosé de Brignolles
marble top
83.2 × 126.4 × 61.9 cm
(2 ft. 8¾ in. × 4 ft. 1¼ in.
× 2 ft. ⅜ in.)
72.DA.63.1 – .2

The design of this ornately carved German commode
and its pair was influenced by the engravings of François de Cuvilliés (circa 1695 – 1768), architect for the
Elector of Bavaria and one of the leading interpreters
of the Rococo style.

CARTONNIER
AND CLOCK

Cartonnier made by Bernard II
van Risenburgh (b. after
1696–circa 1766, master
before 1730); clock movement
made by Étienne II Le Noir
(1699–1778, master 1717);
the name of the maker of the
clock case is unknown; dial
enameled by Jacques Decla
(active 1742–d. after 1764)
French (Paris), circa 1740–46
Oak and poplar veneered
with alder, amaranth, and
cherry and painted with *vernis
Martin*; gilt-bronze mounts;
enameled metal dial; painted
bronze figures; glass
192 × 103 × 41 cm
(6 ft. 3⅝ in. × 3 ft. 4⁹⁄₁₆ in.
× 1 ft. 4⅛ in.)
83.DA.280

The *cartonnier* is stamped B.V.R.B. for the cabinetmaker
Bernard II van Risenburgh. The pigeonholes in the
central section and the narrow cupboards at the sides of
the base were intended to contain papers. The black
and gold decoration is of *vernis Martin*, a French imitation of Oriental lacquer named after the Martin brothers, who excelled in this technique. In the Rococo
period the use of Japanese or Chinese lacquer panels to
decorate furniture was popular; however, the exotic
lacquer was expensive for the client and difficult to
obtain, so Parisian craftsmen learned to imitate it. The
back of the clock dial is dated 1746.

One of a Pair of Wall Lights

French (Paris), 1745 – 49
Gilt bronze
72.4 × 47.6 × 26.7 cm
(2 ft. 4½ in. × 1 ft. 6¾ in.
× 10½ in.)
89.DF.26.1 –.2

Boldly sculptural, these wall lights
are massive in scale and form. They
undoubtedly were designed for a
formal interior, probably en suite with
other wall lights and a chandelier.
The name of the maker is not known.

Commode

Attributed to Jean-Pierre Latz
(circa 1691 – 1754)
French (Paris), circa 1745 – 49
Oak and poplar veneered
with *bois satiné*; walnut
drawers; gilt-bronze mounts;
fleur de pêcher marble top
87.7 × 151.5 × 65 cm
(2 ft. 10½ in. × 4 ft. 11⅞ in.
× 2 ft. 2⅝ in.)
83.DA.356

Although this commode is not stamped with a cabinetmaker's name, it can be firmly attributed to Latz since
his stamp is found on a commode of precisely the same
design now in the Palazzo Quirinale, Rome. That commode was taken to Italy in 1753 by Louise-Elisabeth,
a daughter of Louis XV, who had married Philip,
Duke of Parma (reigned 1748 – 1765), son of Philip V
of Spain (reigned 1700–1746).

One of a Pair of Cabinets

Made by Bernard II van Risenburgh (b. after 1696 – circa 1766, master before 1730)
French (Paris), circa 1745 – 50
Oak veneered with *bois satiné*, kingwood, and cherry; gilt-bronze mounts
149 × 101 × 48.3 cm
(4 ft. 10⅞ in. × 3 ft. 3¼ in. × 1 ft. 7 in.)
84.DA.24.1 – .2

Stamped B.V.R.B. (see p. 205), this low cabinet and its pair are of unique form and were probably used to hold small objets d'art such as porcelains and bronzes or natural curiosities such as shells, minerals, and coral. The cabinets are too deep to use for books. A slide, situated beneath the upper doors, can be pulled out and may have been used by the owner while rearranging and studying his collection.

Compound Microscope with Case

French (Paris), circa 1751
Microscope: gilt bronze; glass and mirror glass; enamel; shagreen
Case: wood; gilded leather; brass closing fixtures; original lining of silk velvet with silver braid; slides of various natural specimens and brass implements
Microscope: 48 × 28 × 20.5 cm
(1 ft. 6⅞ in. × 11 in. × 8¹⁄₁₆ in.)
Case: 66 × 34.9 × 27 cm
(2 ft. 2 in. × 1 ft. 1¼ in. × 10⅝ in.)
86.DH.694

This microscope was made for a noble dilettante scientist who would have used it in his *laboratoire* or *cabinet de curiosités* to explore the mysteries of the natural world being revealed during the Age of Enlightenment.

A microscope of the same form, known to have belonged to Louis XV, was kept in his *observatoire* at the Château de La Muette. The Museum's example is still in working condition. A drawer in the case holds extra lenses and eighteenth- and nineteenth-century specimen slides of such items as a geranium petal, hair, and a flea.

Corner Cupboard

Made by Jacques Dubois (circa 1694–1763, master 1742); clock movement made by Étienne II Le Noir (1699–1778, master 1717); dial enameled by Antoine-Nicolas Martinière (1706–1784, master 1720)
French (Paris), circa 1744–55
Oak, mahogany, and spruce veneered with *bois satiné* and kingwood; enameled metal clock dial; gilt-bronze mounts; glass
289.5 × 129.5 × 72 cm
(9 ft. 6 in. × 4 ft. 3 in. × 2 ft. 4½ in.)
79.DA.66

This cupboard, stamped I. DUBOIS, was ordered by the dealer Lullier of Warsaw for Count Jan Clemens Branicki, the head of the Polish army. It was delivered to him in Warsaw, and an inventory of the contents of his *hôtel* shows that it stood in a grand *salon* as a pendant to a large ceramic stove. Of unique form, the cupboard is based on a print of a drawing by the great Rococo ornamentalist Nicolas Pineau. The back of the clock dial is dated 1744.

DOUBLE DESK

Made by Bernard II van
Risenburgh (b. after
1696–circa 1766, master
before 1730)
French (Paris), circa 1750
Oak and mahogany veneered
with tulipwood, kingwood,
and *bois satiné*; gilt-bronze
mounts
107.8 × 158.7 × 84.7 cm
(3 ft. 6½ in. × 5 ft. 2½ in.
× 2 ft. 9⅜ in.)
70.DA.87

The form of this massive desk, stamped B.V.R.B. (see
pp. 205 and 207), is unique. Flaps let down on both
sides to form writing surfaces, revealing pigeonholes
and drawers. The desk was acquired by the Duke of
Argyll in the nineteenth century and remained in his
family until it was acquired by J. Paul Getty.

BED (*LIT À LA TURQUE*)

Attributed to Jacques-Jean-
Baptiste Tilliard (1723–1798,
master 1752)
French (Paris), circa 1750–60
Gessoed and gilded beech
and walnut; modern silk
upholstery
174 × 264.8 × 188 cm
(5 ft. 8½ in. × 8 ft. 8¼ in.
× 6 ft. 2 in.)
86.DA.535

This large bed, known as a *lit à la turque*, was undoubtedly made for a large *chambre à coucher* in a fashionable grand hôtel. It would have been placed against the
wall, with a draped baldachin above. It is a masterpiece of its kind, unequaled in size, and the quality of
the carving and gilding in two colors is particularly
extravagant. Two smaller but similarly monumental and
sculptural beds exist; both are stamped Tilliard. One
is in Versailles and belonged at one point to Madame du
Barry, a mistress of Louis XV.

COMMODE

Attributed to Joseph
Baumhauer (d. 1772)
French (Paris), circa 1750
Oak veneered with ebony;
set with panels of Japanese
lacquer on Japanese arborvitae,
painted with *vernis Martin*;
gilt-bronze mounts; *campan
mélangé vert* marble top
88.3 × 146.1 × 62.6 cm
(2 ft. 10¾ in. × 4 ft. 9½ in.
× 2 ft. ⅝ in.)
55.DA.2

The front and sides of this commode are set with
panels of Japanese lacquer, the seams of which are hid-
den under the mounts. The remaining surfaces are
painted in imitation of *nashiji*, a clear lacquer sprinkled
with gold. This commode bears the trade label of the
eighteenth-century furniture dealer François-Charles
Darnault.

BUST OF LOUIS XV OF FRANCE

French, Mennecy manu-
factory, circa 1750–55
Soft-paste porcelain
43.2 × 24.5 × 14.5 cm
(1 ft. 5 in. × 9⁹/₁₆ in. × 5¹¹/₁₆ in.)
84.DE.46

In 1734 the duc de Villeroy established a
soft-paste porcelain manufactory, which
after 1748 was located at Mennecy.
Because of the difficulties of firing large
pieces of porcelain in the kilns, this
bust of the king was made in two pieces,
joined above the crown on the plinth.
The plinth is decorated with an asym-
metrical Rococo cartouche (enclosing
the French royal coat of arms) and with
military trophies.

ONE OF A SET OF FOUR WALL LIGHTS

Made by François-Thomas
Germain (1726–1791)
French (Paris), 1756
Gilt bronze
99.6 × 63.2 × 41 cm
(3 ft. 3¼ in. × 2 ft. ⅞ in.
× 1 ft. 4⅛ in.)
81.DF.96.1–.4

Signed by François-Thomas Germain,
silversmith to the king (see p. 204),
these large, late Rococo wall lights were
finished with an unusually high degree
of attention to their casting and gilding.
The lights were commissioned by the
duc d'Orléans for his residence in Paris,
the Palais Royal. Later in the eighteenth
century they were bought by Louis XIV
(reigned 1774–1792) and hung in
rooms used by Marie-Antoinette in the
Château de Compiègne.

READING AND WRITING STAND

Made by Abraham Roentgen
(1711–1793)
German (Neuwied-am-
Rhein), circa 1760–65
Pine, oak, and walnut
veneered with rosewood,
alder, palisander, ivory,
ebony, and mother-of-pearl;
gilded metal fittings
76.8 × 71.7 × 48.8 cm
(2 ft. 6½ in. × 2 ft. 4½ in.
× 1 ft. 7¼ in.)
85.DA.216

The top of this stand is inlaid with the coat of arms of Johann Philipp von Walderdorff, Prince Archbishop and Elector of Trier. Walderdorff was Roentgen's most important patron, and in the 1750s and 1760s, the latter delivered some twenty pieces of elaborate furniture to Walderdorff's palace. This stand is fitted with numerous concealed drawers that open at the press of a button or turn of a key.

LIDDED
BULB VASE

French, Niderviller
manufactory,
circa 1768
Hard-paste porcelain,
polychrome enamel
decoration, and gilding
17 × 19.5 × 11 cm
(6¼ in. × 7¾ in. × 4¼ in.)
99.DE.11

This vase is painted with the coat of arms of its original
owner, a German noble, Christian Moritz Eugen Franz,
Graf zu Königsegg. On the front of the vase are the
initials J.D., possibly for the painter Joseph Deutsch,
who began working at the Niderviller porcelain manufactory about 1768. The back is painted with the
factory mark, a monogram BN for Beyerlé Niderviller.
Jean-Louis Beyerlé (1709–1786) established a ceramics
manufactory at Niderviller in Lorraine. It produced
hard-paste porcelain from 1759 until 1770, when the
manufactory was sold. The interior of the vase was once
fitted with a tray to support flowering bulbs. When not
in use, the vase was purely decorative.

ONE OF A PAIR OF VASES

Painting attributed to
Charles-Nicolas Dodin
(1734–1803)
French, Sèvres manufactory,
circa 1760
Soft-paste porcelain, pink,
green, and *bleu lapis* ground
colors, polychrome enamel
decoration, and gilding
29.8 × 16.5 × 14.6 cm
(11¾ × 6½ × 5¾ in.)
78.DE.358.1–.2

The lower sections of this vase and its
pair were designed to hold small flowering bulbs, while the tall central section
was intended to hold potpourri, the
scent of which would emanate through
the pierced trellis at the top. Such vases
would have formed a garniture with
others of various shapes (see p. 214).
Chinoiserie scenes are rare on Sèvres
porcelain, and it is even more rare
to find three ground colors (pink, green,
and dark blue) on one piece. Each color
required a separate firing of the fragile
porcelain. From archival records it is
known that these vases come from a set
purchased by Madame de Pompadour,
mistress of Louis XV, from the Sèvres
manufactory in 1760.

LIDDED POTPOURRI VASE

Painting attributed to
Charles-Nicolas Dodin
(1734–1803)
French, Sèvres manufactory,
circa 1760
Soft-paste porcelain, pink
and green ground colors,
polychrome enamel
decoration, and gilding
37.5 × 34.8 × 17.4 cm
(1 ft. 2¾ in. × 1 ft. 1¹¹⁄₁₆ in.
× 6¹³⁄₁₆ in.)
75.DE.11

This *vase vaisseau à mât*, or boat-shaped vase, was
designed to contain scented potpourri—dried flower
petals and herbs—and its lid is pierced to allow the
scent to permeate the air. The painted genre scene on
the front is surrounded by a ground of pink and green.
The gold fleurs-de-lis on the pennant draped around
the "mast" suggest royal ownership. This soft-paste
porcelain vase is one of the rarest and most elaborate of
Rococo models produced in the French royal porcelain manufactory at Sèvres. Such vases were intended
to be sold with others of various shapes to form a
matching set, or garniture.

Writing and Toilet Table

Made by Jean-François Oeben
(1721–1763, master 1761)
French (Paris), circa 1754
Oak veneered with king-
wood, amaranth, tulipwood,
and other stained and
natural exotic woods; leather;
silk; gilt-bronze mounts
71.1 × 80 × 42.8 cm
(2 ft. 4 in. × 2 ft. 7½ in.
× 1 ft. 4⅞ in.)
71.DA.103

The top of this table of multiple uses slides back, and
a drawer unit can be pulled forward, revealing another
sliding top concealing compartments lined with blue
watered silk. These elaborate mechanisms and the fine
floral and trellised marquetry decorating it are trademarks of the table's maker, the royal *ébéniste* Jean-
François Oeben. Cosmetic pots and writing materials
would have been kept in this table and its surfaces used
for writing.

ONE OF A PAIR OF VASES

After an engraving by
Benigno Bossi (1727 – 1792)
of a design by Ennemond-
Alexandre Petitot
(1727 – 1801)
French (Paris), circa 1765 – 70
Porphyry; red marble;
gilt-bronze mounts
38.7 × 41 × 27.7 cm
(1 ft. 3¼ in. × 1 ft. 4⅛ in. ×
10⅞ in.)
83.DJ.16.1 – .2

Petitot's thirty designs for fantastic vases were engraved
by Benigno Bossi in 1764, and the publication was dedicated to Guillaume-Leon du Tillot, marquis de Felino,
first minister of the court of Parma. Petitot, a pupil of
Jacques-Germain Soufflot, became architect to the Duke
of Parma in 1753 and remained in Italy for the rest of
his life. The designs were probably intended for stone
garden vases, but here an anonymous *bronzier* working
with a *marbrier* has successfully converted the somewhat bizarre invention to ornamental vases suitable for
a classical interior.

LIDDED BOWL
ON STAND

Painted by Pierre-Antoine
Méreaud *l'aîné*
(circa 1735 – 1791)
French, Sèvres manufactory,
1764
Soft-paste porcelain, poly-
chrome enamel decoration,
and gilding
Bowl H: 12.4 cm (4⅞ in);
W: 19.7 cm (7¾ in);
D: 15.2 cm (6 in.);
Stand H: 3.9 cm (1⁹⁄₁₆ in);
DIAM: 21.1 cm (8⁵⁄₁₆ in.)
78.DE.65

Decorated in the restrained transitional style of the
1760s, when the Rococo was giving way to the newly
fashionable Neoclassical taste, this lidded bowl is
painted with the monogram and coat of arms of the
eighth daughter of Louis XV of France, Madame Louise
(see p. 222). The porcelain is painted with the mark
of the painter Méreaud *père* and the date letter I for 1764,
the year Madame Louise is recorded in the archives at
Sèvres as having bought it.

CONSOLE TABLE

After designs by Victor Louis
(1737 – 1807); table attributed
to Pierre Deumier
(active from the 1760s)
French (Paris), circa 1765 – 70
Silvered and gilt bronze;
bleu turquin marble top
83.5 × 129.5 × 52 cm
(2 ft. 8⅞ in. × 4 ft. 3 in.
× 1 ft. 8½ in.)
88.DF.118

The design of this table follows two drawings — preserved in the University Library, Warsaw — one of
which was made by the French architect Victor Louis.
Louis had been commissioned in 1765 to renovate the
royal palace in Warsaw for Stanislas II Augustus,
King of Poland (reigned 1764 – 1795). A table of this
design was delivered to the palace.

CABINET

Made by Joseph Baumhauer
(d. 1772)
French (Paris), circa 1765
Oak veneered with ebony,
tulipwood, maple, Japanese
cedar, and amaranth; set
with panels of seventeenth-
century Japanese lacquer;
gilt-bronze mounts; jasper top
89.6 × 120.2 × 58.6 cm
(2 ft. 11¼ in. × 3 ft. 11⅛ in.
× 1 ft. 11⅛ in.)
79.DA.58

The design of this early Neoclassical cabinet is severely
architectonic and includes such classical elements
as fluted, canted pilasters and Ionic capitals. Although
fairly simple in appearance, it is made from rare
and expensive materials. The *kijimaki-e* lacquer panels,
sanded so that the grain of the wood shows, are of
very fine quality and of late seventeenth-century date.
A semiprecious hard stone, yellow jasper, was used
for the top instead of less expensive marble.

The cabinet is stamped JOSEPH, the mark of the
cabinetmaker Joseph Baumhauer.

ONE OF A SET OF SIX WALL LIGHTS

Made by Philippe Caffieri
(1714–1774, master 1743)
French (Paris), circa 1765–70
Gilt bronze
64.8 × 41.9 × 31.1 cm
(2 ft. 1½ in. × 1 ft. 4½ in.
× 1 ft. ¼ in.)
78.DF.263.1–.4; 82.DF.35.1–.2

Signed gilt-bronze objects such as this are rare since the craftsmen who made them only occasionally put their names on their work. This light is further documented by a drawing signed by Philippe Caffieri and depicting the same model. These wall lights are after a design, possibly by Caffieri himself, made in 1768 for the redecoration of one of the residences of the King of Poland.

MANTEL CLOCK

Case by Étienne Martincourt
(d. 1791, master 1762);
movement made by Étienne-
Augustin Le Roy (1737–
1792, master 1758)
French (Paris), circa 1772
Gilt bronze; enameled metal;
glass
66 × 59.7 × 32.4 cm
(2 ft. 4 in. × 1 ft. 11½ in.
× 1 ft. ¼ in.)
73.DB.78

Known from documents to have belonged to Louis XVI, this clock is a remarkable work of casting, since details like the rosettes in the trellis were cast together with the elements they decorate. The usual practice was to cast all of these pieces separately. Although the clock, which came from the Palais des Tuileries, does not bear the name of its maker, a drawing for it by the *bronzier* Étienne Martincourt is known. The female figures flanking the urn represent Astronomy and Geography.

One of a Pair of Lidded Vases

Painted reserves attributed to Jean-Baptiste-Étienne Genest (active 1752–1789) French, Sèvres manufactory, circa 1768–69 Soft-paste porcelain, *bleu Fallot* ground color, grisaille enamel decoration, and gilding; gilt-bronze mounts 45.1 × 24.1 × 19.1 cm (1 ft. 5¼ in. × 9½ in. × 7½ in.) 86.DE.520.1–.2

This vase is of nearly unique form. The grisaille reserves and the pale blue ground strewn with gilded dots create a subtle finish markedly different from the strong, brightly colored decoration frequently employed at the Sèvres porcelain manufactory in the later eighteenth century.

COMMODE

Made by Gilles Joubert
(1689–1775)
French (Paris), 1769
Oak veneered with king-
wood, tulipwood, holly,
bois satiné, and ebony; gilt-
bronze mounts; *sarrancolin*
marble top
93.5 × 181 × 68.5 cm
(3 ft. ¾ in. × 5 ft. 11¼ in.
× 2 ft. 3 in.)
55.DA.5

This commode was delivered in 1769 to Versailles for
use in the bedchamber of Madame Louise, daughter of
Louis XV (see p. 218). It is inscribed on the back with
the number 2556, identifying it in the royal inventories.
Gilles Joubert, best known for his Rococo work, ven-
tured to design this commode in the newly fashionable
Neoclassical style.

SECRÉTAIRE

Made by Philippe-Claude
Montigny (1734–1800,
master 1766)
French (Paris), circa 1770–75
Oak veneered with *bois satiné*,
tortoiseshell, brass, pewter,
and ebony bandings; gilt-
bronze mounts
141.5 × 84.5 × 40.3 cm
(4 ft. 7½ in. × 2 ft. 9 in.
× 1 ft. 3¼ in.)
85.DA.378

The front and sides of this Neoclassical *secrétaire-à-
abattant* are covered with large marquetry panels
of tortoiseshell, brass, and pewter dating from the late
seventeenth century. They originally were tabletops
that were reused by Montigny, who was well known as
a specialist in this type of work. The reuse of such
old panels or the making of new ones was fashionable
during the late eighteenth century among the most
advanced connoisseurs. This vogue is known as the
"boulle revival" after the technique's greatest seventeenth-century practitioner, André-Claude Boulle.

It is unusual to find an eighteenth-century prove-
nance for nonroyal furniture. Two previous owners—
both courtiers at Versailles—have been identified for
this *secrétaire*.

ONE OF A SET OF FOUR TAPESTRIES

Woven under the direction of
Michel Audran (1701–1771)
and his son Jean Audran *fils*
(active 1771–1794)
French, Gobelins manu-
factory, 1770–72
Wool and silk;
modern cotton lining
371 × 507.5 cm
(12 ft. 2 in. × 16 ft. 7 in.)
82.DD.67

Entitled *The Feast of Sancho on the Island of Barataria*,
this tapestry is from a set of four depicting various
scenes from Cervantes's *Don Quixote* that was woven
at the Gobelins manufactory. They make up one of
many similar sets woven between 1763 and 1787 after
cartoons by the painter Charles Coypel (1694–1752).
The designs of the elaborate frames and surrounds
were altered periodically as styles changed. Such tapestries were often presented by the French king to roy-
alty and nobility from other countries in Europe. This
set was given by Louis XVI to the Duke and Duchess
of Saxe-Teschen, who were traveling in France in
1786 (the duchess was the sister of Marie-Antoinette).

A number of examples from the *Don Quixote* series
exist, but the Museum's tapestries are unusual in that
the colors remain relatively unfaded and retain many of
the softer hues now lost on other examples.

SECRÉTAIRE

Made by Martin Carlin (circa
1730–1785, master 1766)
French (Paris) and Sèvres
manufactory, circa 1776–77
Oak veneered with tulipwood
and amaranth veneered with
holly; soft-paste porcelain
plaques with polychrome
enamel decoration and gilding; enameled metal; gilt-
bronze mounts; marble top
107.9 × 103 × 35.5 cm
(3 ft. 6¼ in. × 3 ft. 4½ in.
× 1 ft. 2 in.)
81.DA.80

The upright *secrétaire*, a type of writing desk, came into
fashion in the mid-eighteenth century. The fall front of
this example lowers to form a writing surface, revealing
drawers and pigeonholes. This Neoclassical *secrétaire* is
decorated with flower-painted Sèvres porcelain plaques,
an expensive fashion introduced by the Parisian furniture dealers in the 1770s. Its unusually small size suggests that the desk was made for a bedroom.

GARNITURE OF THREE VASES

Models designed by Jacques-François Deparis (active 1746–1797); at least one vase finished by Étienne-Henry Bono (active 1754–1781); reserves painted by Antoine Caton (active 1749–1798); gilding by Étienne-Henry Le Guay (1719/20–circa 1799); jeweling by Philippe Parpette (active 1755–1806)
French, Sèvres manufactory, 1781
Soft-paste porcelain, *beau bleu* ground color, polychrome enamel decoration, enamel imitating jewels, gilding, and gold foil
40.8 × 24.8 × 18.4 cm
(1 ft. 4 in. × 9¾ in. × 7¼ in.);
49.6 × 27.7 × 19.3 cm
(1 ft. 6½ in. × 10⅞ in. ×
7⅞ in.); 40.5 × 25.4 × 18.3 cm
(1 ft. 3¹⁵⁄₁₆ in. × 10 in. × 7³⁄₁₆ in.)
84.DE.718.1–.3

This set of lavishly decorated vases (along with a similar pair now in the Walters Art Gallery, Baltimore) formed a *garniture de cheminée* that was purchased by Louis XVI on November 2, 1781, and placed in his library at Versailles. These vases, prime examples of the mature Neoclassical style at Sèvres, are among the most fully documented works of porcelain in the Museum's collection. Known as a *vase des âges*, this shape was produced at Sèvres from 1778 in three sizes that differ in the rendering of the "handles": bearded male heads for the largest size, female heads for the middle size, and boys' heads for the small size (in Baltimore). The oval reserves on the front of each vase were painted in polychrome enamels with scenes based on engravings by Jean-Baptiste Tilliard (circa 1740–1813) after designs by Charles Monnet (1732–after 1808). These engravings illustrated an edition of one of Louis XVI's favorite books, *Les Aventures de Télémaque*.

These vases are among the largest pieces of jeweled porcelain made at Sèvres. The procedure was exceptionally expensive and demanded great skill. It is clear that only the factory's most experienced and accomplished decorators were involved in producing this garniture. No directly comparable sets of vases are known.

ROLLTOP DESK

Attributed to David Roentgen
(1743 – 1807, master 1780);
some gilt-bronze mounts by
François Rémond (circa
1747– 1812, master 1774)
German (Neuwied-am-
Rhein), 1787 – 88
Oak, fir, and Scots pine
veneered with mahogany
and maple burl; gilt-bronze
mounts; steel fittings
168.3 × 155.9 × 89.3 cm
(5 ft. 6¼ in. × 5 ft. 1⅜ in.
× 2 ft. 11⅛ in.)
72.DA.47

Made in the Neoclassical style, this desk is one of several made by Roentgen, many of which were purchased
by Catherine the Great (reigned 1762 – 1796). When
the writing surface is pulled out, a mechanism automati-
cally withdraws the solid rolltop back into the carcass,
displaying the drawers and pigeonholes inside the
desk. It is also fitted with both a reading stand and a
writing-surface unit, which could be used by a person standing at the closed desk. This unit is concealed,
folded, behind the gilt-bronze plaque; it projects forward when the weight-driven mechanism is activated
by the turn of a key. Roentgen specialized in furniture
with such elaborate mechanical fittings.

ONE OF A PAIR OF CANDELABRA

Attributed to Pierre-Philippe
Thomire (1751–1843, master
1772) after designs by Louis-
Simon Boizot (1743–1809)
French (Paris), circa 1785
Gilt and patinated bronze;
white and *griotte* marbles
H: 83.2 cm (2 ft. 10¼ in.);
DIAM: 29.2 cm (11½ in.)
86.DF.521.1–.2

Although the name of the maker is unknown, this pair of candelabra has been
attributed on stylistic grounds to the
greatest *bronzier* of the late eighteenth
and early nineteenth centuries, Pierre-
Philippe Thomire. A drawing in the
Musée des Arts Décoratifs (Paris) shows
one of the candelabra displayed on a
fireplace with other objects, including a
clock with vestal virgins and a small
bronze figure of a reading girl on a lamp
base. The clock has always been attributed to Thomire as has the figure, which
was designed by Louis-Simon Boizot
in 1780 for the Sèvres manufactory. It is
known that Thomire did not personally
produce designs for his work, calling
instead on the best-known designers
of his period. It is therefore possible that
Boizot was responsible for the design of
this candelabrum.

BED (*LIT À LA POLONAISE*)

French (Paris), circa 1775–80
Gessoed, gilded, and painted
walnut; gilded iron; modern
silk upholstery and *passementerie*; ostrich feathers
302 × 179 × 226 cm
(9 ft. 11 in. × 5 ft. 10½ in.
× 7 ft. 5 in.)
94.DA.72

This type of grand, formal bed was meant to occupy a
deep recess in the most important bedroom of a private
residence, where visitors were received in the morning.
It is not known who designed the bed, who executed
the frame, or for whom it was made. The head and foot
rails are carved as cornucopia, each overflowing with
fruit, flowers, sheaves of wheat, and nuts. A repeating
pattern of oak leaves and acorns decorate the vertical
posts. The modern upholstery and *passementerie* (fringes,
cords, and tassels) follow the designs of the *ornemaniste*
Richard de Lalonde (active 1780s–90s) and historical
photographs of the bed dating from the early twentieth
century, when it still retained its original hangings.

ONE OF A SET OF FOUR WALL LIGHTS

Model by Claude-Jean Pitoin
(master 1778), casting
attributed to Louis-Gabriel
Féloix (1729–1812)
French (Paris), 1781
Gilt bronze
55.9 × 25.4 × 11.4 cm
(1 ft. 10 in. × 10 in. × 4½ in.)
99.DF.20.1 –.4

This finely chased wall light represents the bounty
of the harvest season through the symbols of the central
shaft as the rod (*thyrsus*) of Bacchus, the god of wine,
and its branches in the form of cornucopias overflowing
with fruit, flowers, and leaves. The set was delivered by
Pitoin to the Château de Versailles in 1781 to illuminate
a small, private room, called the *Cabinet de la Méridi-
enne*, of Marie-Antoinette (1755–1793). She withdrew
to this room at midday to rest while pregnant with
her second child, a son named Louis, who was born in
the autumn of that year.

CABINET

Gilt-bronze mounts cast by Forestier (either Étienne-Jean, master 1764, or his brother Pierre-Auguste, 1755 – 1835) and Badin (active last quarter of the eighteenth century) from models by Gilles-François Martin (circa 1713 – 1795), chased by Pierre-Philippe Thomire (1751 – 1843, master 1772) and gilded by Claude Galle (1759 – 1815); marble top supplied by Lanfant

Made by Guillaume Benneman (d. 1811, master 1785)
Cabinet: French (Paris), 1788
Plaques: seventeenth and eighteenth centuries
Oak veneered with mahogany, ebony, and lacquer *pietre dure* plaques; gilt-bronze mounts; *bleu turquin* marble top
92.2 × 165.4 × 64.1 cm
(3 ft. ¼ in. × 5 ft. 5⅛ in. × 2 ft. 1¼ in.)
78.DA.361

This cabinet was created for the bedroom of Louis XVI at the Château de Saint-Cloud. The *pietre dure* plaques replace the original lacquer panels, which were taken off sometime after the Revolution. One of a pair, the other cabinet is now in the royal palace in Madrid.

CARVED RELIEF

By Aubert-Henri-Joseph
Parent (1753 – 1835)
French (Paris), 1789
Limewood
69.4 × 47.9 × 6.2 cm
(2 ft. 3⅛ in. × 1 ft. 6⅞ in.
× 2⅜ in.)
84.SD.76

This virtuoso display piece was made as both a work
of art and as a demonstration of the maker's skill in the
art of carving. It is made from a single piece of limewood. The maker of this piece, Aubert Parent, is best
known for still-life reliefs carved in fruitwoods. Parent
came to prominence in 1778 when he began working
for the French Crown. He had already traveled to Italy,
where he may have seen the work of Giuseppe Bonza-
nigo (1744 – 1820), a famous woodcarver from Turin.
After the French Revolution, he left France to work
in Berlin.

Prominent elements in the decoration of this relief
exhibit the interest in Roman antiquity that was an
important element in the Neoclassical style. The tablet
in the center of the vase representing a grasshopper in a
chariot drawn by a parrot is inspired by an engraving
reproducing a fragment of a wall painting found in the
excavations of Herculaneum. On the rectangular plinth
beneath the vase are represented a pair of Loves (putti)
with their torches reversed. A putto with a reversed
torch was a traditional Roman symbol of mourning and
is commonly found on ancient Roman sarcophagi.

CHANDELIER

Made by Gérard-Jean Galle
(1788–1846)
French (Paris), circa 1818–20
Gilt bronze; enameled metal;
glass
H: 129.5 cm (4 ft. 3 in.)
DIAM: 96.5 cm (3 ft. 2 in.)
73.DH.76

The design of this chandelier resembles a hot-air
balloon, such as was launched by the brothers Joseph-
Michel and Jacques-Étienne Montgolfier from the
grounds of the Château de Versailles in 1783. The large
blue enameled globe at the center of the chandelier is
painted with gold stars and encircled by a gilt-bronze
band fitted with the signs of the zodiac; six of the
eighteen candleholders are in the form of winged
griffins. When the chandelier was displayed in an 1819
Paris exhibition, Galle described how the glass bowl
suspended below was intended to contain goldfish
swimming in water. The continuous movement of the
fish was meant to give "agreeable recreation to the eye."

Sculpture and Works of Art

The Department of Sculpture and Works of Art was established in 1984. Its primary goal is to build a collection of European sculpture representing the period from the Renaissance to the end of the nineteenth century. Its other aim is to complement the Department of Decorative Arts (responsible for Northern European decorative arts from 1650 to 1900) and to build the Museum's collection of all European decorative arts from the period prior to 1650 and in southern Europe from 1650 to 1900.

The department now has important holdings in Renaissance ceramics and glass, a small number of silver, gold, and other precious metal objects, single examples of early seventeenth-century German and Netherlandish furniture, and Italian furniture ranging from the sixteenth through the nineteenth century. Covering the same time span, the sculpture collection includes important works by Laurana, Antico, Cellini, Giambologna, van der Schardt, Verhulst, Girardon, Houdon, Clodion, Canova, Barye, and Carpeaux.

HISPANO-MORESQUE BASIN

Spanish (Valencia region, Manises), mid-fifteenth century
Tin-glazed and lustered earthenware
H: 10.8 cm (4½ in.);
DIAM: 49.5 cm (19½ in.)
85.DE.441

In the first half of the fifteenth century Moorish potters in Spain produced the finest pottery in Europe. They specialized in highly prized lusterwares like this dish that were exported throughout the Mediterranean. The difficult luster technique—which produces a shimmering effect—was accomplished by firing metal oxides onto ceramic objects in a special "reduction" kiln starved of oxygen.

The center of the dish—known as a *brasero*—is inscribed IHS (Jesus Hominum Salvator), the monogram Saint Bernard of Siena held up for veneration at the end of his sermons. Around the time of his canonization in 1450, the monogram began appearing on works of art, substantiating the dating of this piece to mid-century. The leaf-spray embellishment that extends around the rim and down the sides is composed of leaves of the bryony plant (a tendril-bearing vine), small flowers, and ferns. This motif is mainly found on Hispano-Moresque wares of the second and third quarters of the fifteenth century.

Braseros often were used as serving trenchers, wash basins, or containers for refreshments used to cool wine or stemware, for example.

Drug Jar (Albarello)

Central Italian (possibly
Pesaro), circa 1480
Tin-glazed earthenware
H: 31.5 cm (12⅜ in.);
DIAM (lip): 11.1 cm (4⅜ in.)
84.DE.104

This pharmaceutical jar is decorated with
a banderole label bordered with scrolling
leaves. The interior is covered with a
lead glaze, less expensive than the brilliant tin glazes on the exterior. The
label identifies the original contents as
syrupus acetositatis citriorum, or syrup
of lemon juice, which was used to reduce
inflammations of the viscera, to calm
fevers, to quench thirst, and to counter-
act drunkenness and dizziness. The
vessel's waisted form is appropriate to
its use, since it was easy to remove from
a pharmacy's shelf crowded with similar
containers. The elegant shape and
masterful glaze painting make this piece
one of the finest of this type of fifteenth-
century jars known.

Ewer

Italian (Murano), late
fifteenth or early sixteenth
century
Free-blown colorless glass
with gold leaf and enamel
decoration
H: 27.2 cm (10¹¹/₁₆ in.)
MAX. WIDTH: 19.3 cm (7⅝ in.)
84.DK.512

Originally used as liturgical vessels in
metal, by the fifteenth century ewers
were being produced in glass and used
as table pitchers to serve wine and other
liquids. This example was formed in
four separate parts: spout, handle (both
originally gilt), body, and base. By
the beginning of the sixteenth century,
the enameled scale pattern made of
small dots had become a popular Venetian glass motif. The flame design below
the neck was less common. This piece
is one of only a dozen glass ewers that
have survived intact from the period.

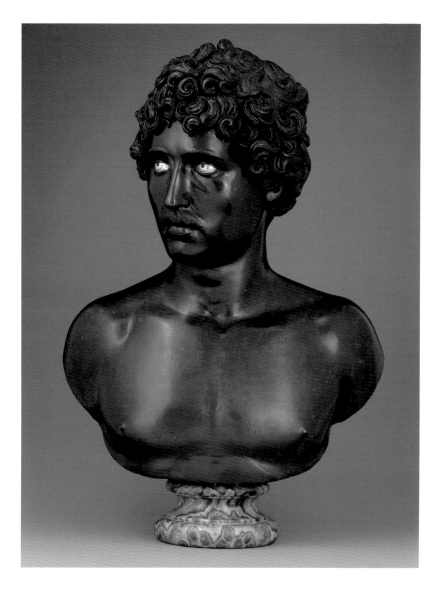

ANTICO

(Pier Jacopo Alari-Bonacolsi)
Italian, circa 1460 – 1528
Bust of a Young Man,
circa 1520
Bronze with silver eyes
54.6 × 45 × 22.3 cm
(21½ × 17¾ × 8¾ in.)
86.SB.688

Trained as a goldsmith, Pier Jacopo became the principal sculptor at the court of Mantua in the late fifteenth
and early sixteenth centuries. He executed many bronze
reductions and variants of famous antiquities, earning
himself the nickname Antico. The Museum's bronze
is one of only seven known busts generally accepted
as being by him. It derives from an ancient marble bust,
now in the Hispanic Society of America, New York.
The use of silver for the eyes emulates a frequent practice of antiquity.

BENVENUTO
CELLINI

Italian, 1500 – 1571
Satyr, cast after a model of
circa 1542
Bronze
H: 56.8 cm (22⅜ in.)
85.SB.69

In 1540 Cellini, a leading sixteenth-
century sculptor, traveled to Fontainebleau to work for King François I.
One of the artist's major commissions
was for the Porte Dorée, the monumental palace entrance ordered by the king
in 1542. The project called for a bronze
lunette depicting the nymph thought to
reside in the forest of Fontainebleau.
It was to be supported by two menacing
satyrs, one on either side of the door,
with winged personifications of Victory
in the spandrels. Although the door-
way never was completed, the Museum's
bronze was cast from Cellini's wax model
for one of the satyrs.

BENVENUTO
CELLINI?

Italian, 1500 – 1571
Hercules Pendant, circa 1540
Gold, enamel (white, blue,
and black), and a baroque
pearl
6 × 5.4 cm (2⅜ × 2⅛ in.)
85.SE.237

A masterpiece of Renaissance jewelry,
this pendant can be associated with
the court of François I (reigned 1515 –
1547) at Fontainebleau. The subject,
Hercules with the columns of Cadiz,
was one of many such Herculean images
utilized by the king in royal commissions. The pendant's style and unusual
sculptural quality recall the work of the
Italian sculptor Benvenuto Cellini,
who was employed at Fontainebleau from
1540 to 1545 (see entry at left).

ITALIAN ARTIST
WORKING AT
FOUNTAINBLEAU,
FRANCE

Pair of Andirons in the Form
of a Nymph and a Satyr,
circa 1540–45
Bronze
Nymph: 85.1 × 39 × 14 cm
(33½ × 15¼ × 5½ in.)
Satyr: 82 × 39.5 × 13 cm
(32¼ × 15½ × 5 in.)
94.SB.77.1–.2

On the basis of the Mannerist style of the figures, these andirons—the fireplace equipment that supports wood in a hearth—can be dated about 1540 to 1545. This date is supported by the fact that each figure holds in an urn above its head a salamander, the personal emblem of the French king François I (reigned 1515–1547). It seems likely that they were executed for François I by one of the many Italian artists who had been brought to France to work at the king's château at Fontainebleau. These two objects are among the very few small bronzes that can be associated with Fontainebleau, and they appear to be the earliest known figural andirons. The twisted pose, vigorous musculature, and emotional expressiveness of the male figure have many points in common with Rosso's designs for sculptures and paintings in the Gallery of François I (1534–40), while the elongated, mannered proportions and chilly, detached classicism of the female figure evoke Primaticcio's stuccoed caryatids in the Chamber of Madame d'Étampes (1541–44).

BERNARD PALISSY

French, 1510(?)–1589/90
Oval Basin, circa 1550
Lead-glazed earthenware
48.2 × 36.8 cm (19 × 14½ in.)
88.DE.63

Palissy was a man of many interests and talents who, in addition to being a geologist, chemist, philosopher, and ceramist, was also an outspoken Huguenot imprisoned for his involvement in the Protestant riots of the mid-sixteenth century. His subsequent freedom and protection were due to the efforts of his influential Catholic patrons such as Anne de Montmorency and Catherine de' Medici. As a ceramist, Palissy produced his distinctive pottery, called rustic ware, by making life-casts of crustaceans, plants, and reptiles and attaching these casts to traditional ceramic forms. He then naturalistically decorated these wares, as on this example, with lead-based glazes that would melt into one another when fired in the kiln, increasing the realism of the river-like scenes. This basin is exceptional not only for the subtle modeling of its surface—with attention given to the most minute details and surface textures—but also for its unusual ground color; it is one of only three works by Palissy with similar light-colored grounds (that is, white or yellow). The great majority of Palissy wares have backgrounds colored either dark brown or blue. Palissy's rustic works were so popular that they were imitated during his own lifetime and copied in the nineteenth century by such notable ceramic manufactories as Sèvres in France and Wedgwood in England.

**ORAZIO FONTANA
OR HIS WORKSHOP**

Italian, 1510 – 1571
Basin with Deucalion and
Pyrrha, circa 1565 – 71
Tin-glazed earthenware
H: 6.3 cm (2½ in.);
DIAM: 46.3 cm (18½ in.)
86.DE.539

One of the most active, innovative ceramists of his
time, Orazio helped develop a new genre of maiolica
decoration with elegant grotesque motifs. The central
medallion tells the story of a husband and wife who
renewed the human race after a devastating flood by
casting stones behind them that assumed human form
(Ovid, *Metamorphoses* 1:260 – 415).

GIAMBOLOGNA

(Jean Boulogne)
Italo-Flemish, 1529 – 1608
Female Figure (possibly
Venus, formerly called
Bathsheba), 1571 – 73
Marble
H: 115 cm (45¼ in.)
82.SA.37

Giambologna was one of the most innovative sculptors
to experiment with the serpentine figure, the upwardly
spiraling movement that demands to be looked at from
every point of view. The figure's pose conforms to
an ideal, artificial spiral achieved through the graceful
but complicated twisting of limbs. For Giambologna,
a natural stance was less important than the contrast between her long, smooth body and the detailed drapery
folds, armband, and coiffure.

FOOTED BOWL (COPPA)

Italian (Murano), circa 1500
Free-blown chalcedony glass
H: 12.3 cm (4⅞ in.);
DIAM (at lip): 19.7 cm
(7¾ in.);
DIAM (at base): 10.6 cm
(4³⁄₁₆ in.)
84.DK.660

This rare object is one of a small extant group of Renaissance bowls in chalcedony, or agate, glass, so called because of its opaque, marbled appearance, which resembles natural hardstones. Highly prized for the beauty of its colors and as a curiosity, chalcedony glass is an example of the Renaissance revival of antiquity, since vessels of the stone were popular in Roman times.

PILGRIM FLASK

Italian (Florence), Medici
porcelain factory,
circa 1575 – 87
Soft-paste porcelain; blue
underglaze decoration
H: 26.4 cm (10⅛ in.);
W: 20 cm (7⅞ in.);
DIAM (lip): 4 cm (1⁹⁄₁₆ in.)
86.DE.630

One of the rare wares produced in the Medici factory under Francesco I, this flask is among the earliest examples of European porcelain. Although Medici wares often display signs of being experimental this work is an exceptional piece with unusually brilliant color.

Almost certainly a display piece, this flask reflects the influence of contemporary maiolica and metalwork — in its shape and molded side loops — and of Chinese porcelain and Turkish Iznik ware in its stylized floral decoration.

ABRAHAM I PFLEGER

German, active 1558–d. 1605
Ewer and Basin, 1583
German (Augsburg), 1583
Parcel-gilt silver; enameled
plaques; engraving
Ewer H: 25 cm (9⅞ in.);
Basin DIAM: 50.5 cm
(19⅞ in.)
85.DG.33.1–.2

In addition to their practical function—serving perfumed water for guests to wash their hands during a meal—this ewer and basin commemorate the marriage of Maria Fugger to Nikolaus Palffy von Erdöd. The coats of arms of the two families, surmounted by the date and a pair of clasped hands, appear in enameled medallions on the top of the ewer and in the center of the basin, and are engraved underneath it. The Fuggers, the most illustrious of German banking and mercantile families, wanted to form an alliance with the Palffys, since one of the main sources of the Fugger fortunes was their copper mines in the Palffys' native Hungary.

Abraham I Pfleger is recorded as one of the most important goldsmiths of sixteenth-century Augsburg. Few of his works have survived. This ewer and basin reveal a style of unusual purity, restraint, and formal severity.

JOHANN GREGOR VAN DER SCHARDT

Dutch, circa 1530–81
Mercury, circa 1570–76
Bronze
H: 115 cm (45¼ in.)
95.SB.8

Van der Schardt was one of the first sculptors to introduce the Italian Mannerist style into Northern Europe. The influence of Italian and classical statuary on his work can be seen in this bronze *Mercury*, which borrows the pose of the famous *Apollo Belvedere* in Rome. Mercury played a central role in classical mythology as a divine messenger, but Van der Schardt chose to depict this athletic youth's return to the ground. Mercury's left arm is elegantly raised and his eyes follow the movement of his hand as if he were preparing to deliver an announcement from the gods. The academic ideal of eloquence that this figure symbolizes must have appealed to van der Schardt's courtly and bourgeois clientele. This *Mercury* can be traced back to the famous collection of the Nuremberg patrician Paul Praun (1548–1616), who owned numerous terracotta and bronze figures by Van der Schardt.

COVERED *FILIGRANA* BEAKER (*STANGENGLAS*)

Glass: German or Italian (Murano), circa 1550–1600; mounts made by Martin Bair (Augsburg, circa 1676–1734), circa 1685
Free- and mold-blown colorless glass with opaque white (*lattimo*) threads; silver-gilt mounts
H (with lid): 30.5 cm (12 in.); DIAM (at base): 10.1 cm (4 in.)
84.DK.513.1–.2

This *Stangenglas*, or tall, cylindrical, footed drinking glass, displays the remarkable technique of trapping small bubbles between threadlike white canes of glass in a net pattern. Although the fine quality of this so-called *vetro a reticello* is consistent with Venetian production of the late sixteenth century, the form is unmistakably Germanic. Given that many Venetians were working in German glasshouses by the second half of the century, it is possible that this beaker was produced by talented Venetian craftsmen north of the Alps.

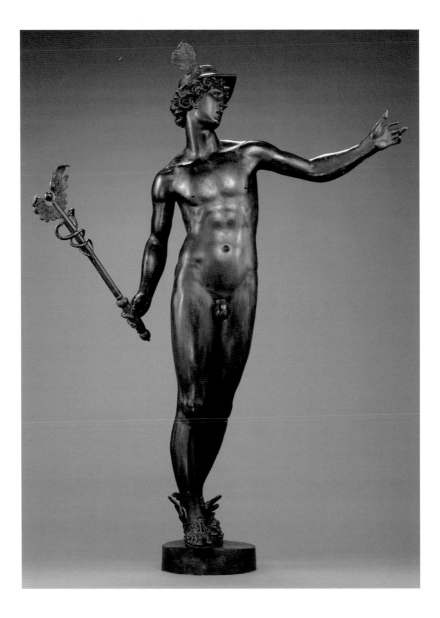

PIETRE DURE
TABLETOP

Italian (Florence or Rome),
Tabletop: circa 1580 – 1600
Base: circa 1825
Tabletop: hard- and soft
stones including lapis lazuli,
coral, rock crystal,
and various types of marble,
breccia, and alabaster
89.9 × 136.5 × 113 cm
(35⅛ × 53¾ × 44½ in.)
92.DA.70

Renaissance Italy, particularly Florence and Rome, witnessed a renewed interest in the ancient art form of stone mosaic. Initially, geometric patterns prevailed, but by the end of the sixteenth century, as the demanding technique was mastered, artists began to include ever more pictorial elements, such as the scrolling foliage on this tabletop. Every decorative element is outlined in white marble, setting off each one from the other and emphasizing the table's jewel-like quality. The inclusion of a particularly rare and beautiful stone — the black, speckled *breccia di Tivoli* in the field surrounding the central oval — indicates the piece must have been made after 1560, the year in which the stone was discovered by Pope Pius IV (reigned 1559 – 1565) in the ruins of the ancient Villa of Quintiliolo at Tivoli. The inclusion of this stone, together with the tabletop's transitional style combining purely geometric with foliate patterns, help date the piece to the last decades of the sixteenth century.

PORTRAIT OF POPE CLEMENT VIII (IPPOLITO ALDOBRANDINI)

Italian, 1600–1
Designed by Jacopo Ligozzi
(Italian, circa 1547–1626)
Executed by Romolo
di Francesco Ferrucci
(del Tadda) (d. 1621)
Marble, lapis lazuli, mother-
of-pearl, limestone,
and calcite (some covering
painted paper or fabric cartouches) on and surrounded
by a silicate black stone
With frame: 101.7 × 75.2 cm
(39¹³⁄₁₆ × 29⅝ in.)
Without frame: 97 × 68 cm
(38³⁄₁₆ × 26¼ in.)
92.SE.67

This hardstone-and-marble mosaic is one of four such portraits ordered by Ferdinando I and produced in his *Galleria de' Lavori in pietre dure*, Florence. The Grand Duke founded this workshop in 1588 so that local craftsmen could be trained to restore ancient objects as well as to create original works in the hardstone medium. The other three portraits depict Cosimo I de' Medici, Henri IV of France (now lost), and Ferdinando I de' Medici (also now lost). The sitter of the Museum's portrait, born Ippolito Aldobrandini, served as Pope Clement VIII from 1592 to 1605. Medici interest in the hardstone medium had been especially intense since the 1580s when Cosimo I began plans to decorate with precious stones a new chapel in the Sacristy of San Lorenzo that would serve as a mausoleum for the grand dukes of Tuscany and their families. The hardstone portraits of Medici family members were probably intended to hang in this chapel as representations of dynastic glory. In addition, these stone portraits, including this one of Clement VIII, exemplified the intrinsic and symbolic power of the stones, the permanence that these stones embody, and the "ingenious artifice" that so characterizes late Mannerism.

DISPLAY CABINET

Flanders (Antwerp?),
early seventeenth century
Walnut and oak veneered
with ebony, tortoiseshell,
coconut(?), and ebonized
wood
210 × 158 × 74.5 cm
(82¼ × 62¼ × 29⅛ in.)
88.DA.10

Antwerp was the most important center for furniture decoration in the Netherlands around the turn of the seventeenth century. As evidence, this cabinet inventively combines architectural forms with fine sculpted figures. The two front doors are decorated with the allegorical figures of Faith and Hope holding their respective attributes of cross and anchor. Charity appears on the front drawer, completing the triad of theological virtues. Behind the four fully sculpted caryatid figures that support the cornice at the very top, a receding cupboard opens to reveal an octagonal mirror surrounded by intricately inlaid geometric patterns.

BASIN WITH SCENES FROM THE LIFE OF CLEOPATRA

Italian (Genoa),
circa 1620–25
Perhaps modeled by
Francesco Fanelli (Italian,
1590[?]–after 1653) after a
sketch by Bernardino
Strozzi (Italian, 1581–1644).
Probably executed by a
Dutch or Flemish silversmith
Silver
DIAM: 75.5 cm (29¾ in.)
85.DG.81

The design of this spectacular basin, executed in exceptionally high relief, is closely based on an oil sketch by the Genoese painter Bernardo Strozzi, now in the Ashmolean Museum, Oxford. It may have been translated into precious metal by a Dutch or Flemish silversmith working in Genoa. As in Strozzi's image, the basin depicts episodes from the story of Anthony and Cleopatra. The organization of these narrative scenes—which include dynamic portrayals of battle, suicide, and death—into concentric bands surrounding a central roundel confirms the basin's Genoese origin.

By the seventeenth century Genoa had become one of the most important Italian centers for the production of precious metalwork, and a great quantity of early Genoese silver must once have existed. Despite this, very few secular examples survive from this period; scarcely more than a dozen of high quality are known. Among these the Museum's basin is the largest and most technically daring in its remarkable depth of relief and precision of chasing.

Throughout his professional life, de Vries seems to have satisfied the dictates of princely taste, for he was courted as a sculptor by some of the most power- ful, discerning patrons of Europe, in- cluding Charles Emmanuel I, Duke of Savoy, and Emperor Rudolf II of Prague (reigned 1576–1612). De Vries worked primarily in bronze, a medium in which he achieved extraordinary virtuosity, and his bronzes are unusual for their consistently high quality and technical sophistication. The *Rearing Horse*— with its smooth musculature, expertly modeled anatomical details, richly colored, reflective surface, and daring balance of the animal's mass on two points—would have merited a promi- nent place in a royal or aristocratic collector's cabinet.

ADRIAEN DE VRIES

Dutch, circa 1560–1626
Rearing Horse, circa 1610–15
Bronze
49.5 × 54.6 × 17.8 cm
(19½ × 21½ × 7 in.)
86.SB.488

ADRIAEN DE VRIES

Dutch, circa 1560–1626
Juggling Man, circa 1615
Bronze
77.2 × 51.8 × 21.9 cm
(30⅜ × 20⅜ × 8⅝ in.)
90.SB.44

Adriaen de Vries received his artistic training in the Florentine workshop of the Mannerist sculptor Giam- bologna (1529–1608). De Vries went on to become the court sculptor to the Duke of Savoy and then to Emperor Rudolf II in Prague. Unlike his teacher, de Vries did not produce multiple versions of his bronzes or allow his models to be cast by other artists. The Museum's *Juggling Man* is therefore a unique compo- sition and one of the sculptor's masterpieces. It was inspired by a Hellenistic marble entitled *Dancing Faun* in the collection of Medici dukes that is now in the Uffizi Gallery, Florence. De Vries changed the details of his prototype significantly: he eliminated the attri- butes of a tail and horns, replaced the foot organ with a bellows and the cymbals with plates for juggling. In de Vries's hands the faun has become a serious—but highly animated—depiction of dynamic equilibrium. The *Juggling Man* exhibits characteristics of de Vries's male figures, including the expressionistic treatment of the hair and musculature, a pointed chin and small mouth, an almost impish facial expression, and promi- nent veins in the feet and hands.

GIANLORENZO BERNINI

Italian, 1598 – 1680
Boy with a Dragon,
circa 1614 – 20
Marble
55.9 × 52 × 41.5 cm
(22 × 20 × 16 in.)
87.SA.42

Bernini, the greatest, most precocious Baroque sculptor, executed this marble when he was only about sixteen years old. It is described in early inventories as representing the young Hercules with a dragon. Unlike its antique precedents, this sculpture presents an unidealized, life-size urchin who cracks the dragon's jaw not in a heroic struggle but with a very human, mischievous smile. By obscuring the boundary between art and reality, Bernini invites the viewer's psychological interaction with the sculpture. *Boy with a Dragon*, fitted for use as an indoor fountain, most likely was commissioned by Maffeo Barberini (later Pope Urban VIII) to decorate his Roman palace.

WORKSHOP OF
BLAUSIUS
FISTULATOR

German, active 1587–1622
Architectural Scene and
Frame
Plaque: South German,
circa 1630–70
Scagliola
Frame: Italian, 1730–40
Ebonized wood with
gilt-bronze mounts
Plaque: 43.5 × 50 cm
(17⅛ × 19¹¹⁄₁₆ in.)
Frame: 73 × 67 cm
(28¾ × 26⅜ in.)
92.SE.69

Scagliola, a mixture of stucco, glue, and colorants
placed upon a stucco surface, was first developed in
South Germany at the end of the sixteenth century as a
more pictorial and less labor intensive imitation of
stone mosaic. The vibrant polychromy of its precisely
rendered architecture, set against the subtle tonalities
of the foliage and sky, make this plaque an artistic
tour-de-force. The exuberant wood and gilt-bronze
frame displays the arms of Pope Clement XII Corsini
(reigned 1730–40) and may indicate that the earlier
plaque was given to him as a gift during his papal tenure.

GIOVANNI
FRANCESCO SUSINI

Italian, circa 1585–circa 1653
*The Abduction of Helen
by Paris*, 1627
Base: circa 1750
Bronze on an eighteenth-
century gilt-bronze base
With base (whose height is
18.5 cm [47 cm]):
68 × 34.2 × 33.7 cm
(26¾ × 13½ × 13¼ in.)
90.SB.32

Susini learned the art of sculpture and bronze casting
from his uncle Antonio, a close collaborator of the
Medici's official court sculptor Giambologna (1529–
1608). In this bronze, Giovanni Francesco drew upon
Giambologna's influence in choosing a complex composition of struggling figures intended to be viewed from
every angle. Nevertheless, the open spatial relationship of the figures, the concern for realistically depicting Helen's supple flesh, and the sense of a climactic
moment frozen in time all recall the new Baroque style
being practiced in Rome. *The Abduction of Helen*, a
progressive and original work, represents the first
important Florentine response to the Roman Baroque
idiom in sculpture.

**ATTRIBUTED
TO GIOVANNI
BATTISTA
CALANDRA**

Italian, 1586–1644
Portrait of Camillo Rospigliosi,
circa 1630–40
Mosaic in gilt-wood frame
62 × 48.5 cm (24⅛ × 19¹⁄₁₆ in.)
87.SE.132

Partly in response to the Counter-Reformation, the
Paleo-Christian art form of mosaic production was revived in seventeenth-century Rome. Mosaic renderings
were appreciated as "eternal" imitations of paintings,
and this jewel-like portrait, of particular chromatic and
pictorial subtlety, likely copies an unknown painting
by one of the artist's famous contemporaries such
as Andrea Sacchi or Guido Reni. Calandra was perhaps
the greatest mosaicist of his time. His work was favored
by the most important papal and royal patrons such
as members of the Aldobrandini and Barberini families.
A label on its gilt-wood frame, which displays the
lozenges of the Rospigliosi family arms, identifies the
sitter as Camillo Rospigliosi (1600–1669), Knight
Commander of the Order of Santo Stefano and brother
to Pope Clement IX.

DISPLAY CABINET

German (Augsburg),
circa 1620–30
Ebony, chestnut, walnut,
pearwood, and boxwood;
ivory, marble, and semi-
precious stones; enamel;
palm wood and tortoiseshell
Several carvings by
Albert Jansz. Vinckenbrinck
(Dutch, 1604/5–1664/5)
73 × 58 × 59 cm
(28¼ × 22¹¹⁄₁₆ × 23¼ in.)
89.DA.28

This architecturally inspired collector's cabinet was
likely influenced by the projects of Ulrich Baumgartner,
the most prominent Augsburg cabinetmaker of the early
seventeenth century. It displays restrained proportions;
elegantly mannered carving in its so-called Auricular-
style, or earlobe-like, details above the front "doors";
and a sensitive colorism contrasting ebony with semi-
precious stone inlay. All four sides open to reveal
a surprisingly complex series of drawers and compartments. The biblical, mythological, and historical
subjects represented on the inside were executed in a
variety of techniques and materials.

MARCUS HEIDEN

German, active 1618–1664
Covered Standing Cup, 1631
(the figural elements probably
added later in the seventeenth
century)
Lathe-turned and carved ivory
H: 63.5 cm (25 in.)
91.DH.75

This lathe-turned and carved ivory goblet, like others
of this medium and date, was made as a demonstration
of artistic skill to amaze and delight the beholder rather
than to serve as a functional drinking cup. It was probably commissioned by Duke Johann Casimir of Saxe-
Coburg for display in his princely *Kunstkammer*, or
collector's cabinet. Two major innovations in the design
of such ivory goblets were introduced in the seventeenth century, and the Covered Standing Cup reflects
both of them. The first involved the combination of
abstract, lathe-turned forms with robustly modeled
figural elements, and the second introduced an element
of asymmetry and a shifting or zigzagging vertical
axis to heighten the sense of precarious balance. The
Standing Cup, which is signed and dated 1631 under
its base, represents one of the fullest realizations of this
new Baroque style in turned ivory vessels.

FRANÇOIS GIRARDON

French, 1628–1715
Pluto Abducting Proserpine,
cast circa 1693–1710
Bronze
H: 105.1 cm (41⅜ in.)
88.SB.73

Girardon's signed abduction group forms a pair with Gaspard Marsy's *Boreas Abducting Orithyia*, also in the Museum's collection (88.SB.74). Both bronzes are based on models for monumental marble groups commissioned by King Louis XIV to decorate the Parterre d'Eau in the gardens at Versailles. In executing their models, the sculptors faced the artistic challenge of achieving a complex composition viewable from all angles and depicting violent action, all within the boundaries of decorum dictated by the French classicizing style. Their success must have been apparent to contemporary collectors, for bronze reductions of the famous Parterre groups already were in widespread demand by the end of the seventeenth century. Girardon's *Pluto Abducting Proserpine* is the finest and most beautifully patinated of the surviving large casts of his original model.

FERDINANDO TACCA

Italian, 1619–1686
Putto Holding a Shield to His Left, 1650–55
Bronze
65.1 × 53.3 × 46.7 cm
(25⅝ × 21 × 18 in.)
85.SB.70.1

This bronze putto or angel is one of a pair commissioned in 1650 to adorn the high altar of the church of Santo Stefano al Ponte in Florence. It testifies to Ferdinando's importance in the transition of the Florentine sculptural style from the late Mannerism of Giambologna (see p. 243) to the Baroque. The putto's elegant gesture and the sway of his hips are the last remnants of Giambologna's legacy, which Ferdinando inherited along with that master's workshop in the Borgo Pinti. However, the infant's realistic anatomy, the dramatic play of light across the complex surfaces of his hair and drapery, and the resulting sense of animation underscore Tacca's mastery of the Baroque idiom.

FRANCESCO MOCHI

Italian, 1580 – 1654
Tabernacle Door with *The
Crucifixion*, circa 1635 – 40
Gilt bronze
54.3 × 28.8 cm (21¼ × 11⅜ in.)
95.SB.2

The elongated, rectangular shape and large size of this relief—as well as the presence of a keyhole and the remains of a hinge—identify it as the door of a sacrament tabernacle, called a *ciborium*, destined for the high altar of a church. *Ciboria* were used to house the sanctified Eucharist and were often grand in scale, towering as much as fifteen feet above the floor. Mochi has taken the exigencies of this placement into consideration in planning the organization and treatment of the relief. The sharp undercutting of the bold, simple figures makes them readable from the distance between the transept, where worshipers would be gathered, and the altar. In addition, the perspective of the clouds and the foreshortening of the figures achieve illusionistic resolution only when viewed from below.

Mochi has organized the composition hieratically rather than naturalistically, in keeping with the Eucharistic theme and function of the relief. Although the crucified Christ and the kneeling Magdalene presumably occupy the same spatial plane, Christ is depicted in higher relief to underscore his importance and the iconic nature of the portrayal. Another unusual feature of this relief is the extension of the arms of the cross beyond the borders of the image, suggesting an infinite and timeless space for the enactment of this sacred scene.

LUISA ROLDÁN

Spanish, circa 1654 – circa
1704
Saint Ginés de la Jara, 169(2?)
Gilt and polychromed pine
and cedar; glass eyes
H: 175.9 cm (69¼ in.)
85.SD.161

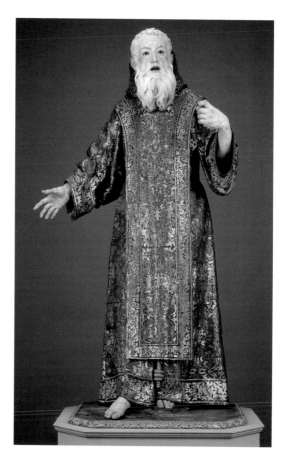

This sculpture of Saint Ginés has been attributed to the
Seville artist Luisa Roldán, known as La Roldana. She
was primarily active in Madrid, where she was named
Sculptor of the Bedchamber (*Escultora de Camara*)
by King Charles II. Indeed, this work displays not only
her exceptionally beautiful and expressive sculptural
style but also an inscription that can be read [LUIS]A
RO[LD]AN, ESC[U]L[TO]RA DE CAMARA AÑO
169[2?]. The rich decoration of the saint's robes is
executed in *estofado*, a technique that simulates the
brocade of ecclesiastic vestments by stamping patterns
of foliage and fleurs-de-lis over brown pigment and
burnished water gilding to mimic the texture and
brilliance of the gold cloth. This sumptuous display,
together with the heightened realism of the *Saint Ginés*,
are typical of the emotionally expressive devotional
practices of Catholic Spain.

NIGHT CLOCK

Giovanni Battista Foggini (Italian, 1652–1725), and Leonard van der Vinne (Flemish, active in Florence, 1650–1713), with bronze figures attributed to Massimiliano Soldani Benzi (Italian, 1658–1740) and clock mechanism by Francesco Papillion (Italian, active circa 1700)

Ebony, gilt bronze, and semi-precious stones including chalcedony, jasper, lapis lazuli, and *verde d'Arno*

95 × 63 × 28 cm

(37⅜ × 24¹⁵⁄₁₆ × 11 in.)

97.DB.37

Popular in seventeenth-century Italy, night clocks were equipped with a small oil lamp that illuminated the dial from behind so that the numbers would be visible in a dark or dimly lighted bedroom. This piece takes the architecturally inspired form of a Baroque altar with the "altarpiece" housing the face of the clock. Combining rare materials, innovative forms, and fine sculpture, this clock is the result of a collaboration among the most skilled artists active in Florence around 1700. Foggini was a major proponent of the late Baroque style in that city, where he also served as court sculptor to Cosimo III, the Grand Duke of Tuscany. He was appointed director of the Medici craft workshops—the Galleria dei Lavori—where he was responsible for developing sculpted

hardstone decoration such as the fruit swags on this clock. At the Galleria, Van der Vinne worked as a cabinet-maker, specializing in masterful intarsias of floral patterns that helped spread the taste for inlay decoration throughout Europe. Soldani Benzi was the finest bronze caster in Europe at the time. The clock's bronze boar copies a Hellenistic marble that was on display at the Uffizi by the middle of the seventeenth century. Around 1700, Soldani Benzi was producing a series of bronze reductions of ancient works in the Uffizi, and this may be a cast of one of them. Little is known of Papillion except that he produced several other clocks and was mentioned in the Florentine clock-makers' guild in 1705.

MASSIMILIANO
SOLDANI BENZI

Italian, 1656–1740
Venus and Adonis,
circa 1715–16
Bronze
46.4 × 49 × 34.2 cm
(18¼ × 19¼ × 13½ in.)
93.SB.4

Massimiliano Soldani Benzi was the
finest bronze caster in late seventeenth-
century Europe and a leading figure
in the evolution of a Florentine Baroque
aesthetic in sculpture. This bronze
group illustrates an episode from Ovid's
Metamorphoses (10:495–739) in which
Adonis, despite the protests of his immortal lover Venus, sets out in pursuit
of a wild boar and is gored to death.
Soldani's interpretation of the narrative emphasizes the poignant tragedy of
the lovers and their final emotional

exchange. Venus, having just arrived on
a cloud, cradles the head of her dying
paramour as she gazes into his eyes. The
figures enact their drama as if on a stage,
in a frontal composition oriented toward
a stationary viewer. This arrangement
recalls contemporary productions of
theater and opera, the latter having been
invented in Florence a century earlier.

Landscape details such as the rocky
ground, flowers, and clouds enhance
the scenographic quality of the bronze.
Other details serve to demonstrate the
artist's superlative skills as a bronze caster. For instance, the leash of Adonis's
hunting dog, which is pulled by a standing cupid, seems to stretch tautly in a
way that defies the rigidity and stasis
inherent to bronze sculpture. By means
of such features in the *Venus and Adonis*,
Soldani proves himself to be a master
of both technique and illusion.

GENNARO LAUDATO

Italian, active 1790s
After a model by
Giuseppe Sanmartino
(Italian, 1720–1793)
*Saint Joseph with the
Christ Child*, 1790s
White-bodied earthenware
(*terraglia*), glazed and
polychromed
H: 54.3 cm (21⅜ in.)
91.SE.74

This work is one of the few examples of eighteenth-century ceramic figures from southern Europe of comparatively large scale, sculptural conception, and brilliant execution. The composition is virtually identical to a life-size marble of the same subject by the Neapolitan sculptor Giuseppe Sanmartino that adorns a niche in the vestibule of the San Cataldo Chapel in the Cathedral of Taranto, Italy. Presumably, the Getty *Saint Joseph with the Christ Child* copies the same terracotta model (now lost) that was used by Sanmartino for his marble figure group in Taranto. The ceramic pair was modeled by Gennaro Laudato, a Neapolitan artist who appears to have been active in the circle of Sanmartino. The stylistic similarities between the Getty *Saint Joseph* and Gennaro Laudato's signed works, such as a ceramic *Tobias and the Angel* based on a drawing by Sanmartino for a silver group in the chapel of the Treasury of San Gennaro, Naples, confirms the attribution of this figure to Laudato.

SIDE TABLE

Italian (Rome), circa 1720–30
Gessoed and gilded lime-
wood; modern marble top
93.9 × 190.5 × 96.5 cm
(47 × 75 × 38 in.)
82.DA.8

This table is carved with masks, deep scrolls, and female heads in keeping with the exuberant, curvaceous forms of the early eighteenth-century Baroque style. It is one of a pair of tables, the other of which is in the Palazzo Barberini, Rome. Although it is not known whether the Barberini table is in its original setting, both pieces undoubtedly were made for one of the grander eighteenth-century palaces in Rome. They probably would have supported works of art—such as bronze sculptures or Chinese porcelains—for display.

FRANCIS HARWOOD

English, active in Florence
1748 – 1783
*Bust of a Man (Possibly
a Boxer or Athlete)*, 1758
Black stone (*pietra da paragone*)
on a yellow Siena marble socle
Bust (with socle):
69.9 × 50.2 × 26.7 cm
(27½ × 19¾ × 10½ in.)
Socle: 12 × 22.2 cm (4¾ × 8¾ in.)
88.SA.114

In contrast to the stereotypical "black-amoor" busts produced in the eighteenth century, this work portrays a specific individual and therefore ranks as one of the earliest European sculpted portraits of a black man. Very little is known of the artist's training. By 1748 he had moved from England to Florence, where he became one of the major sculptors for English aristocrats visiting that city on the Grand Tour. Harwood's classicizing style is rather undistinguished, except for this beautiful and powerful portrait.

SIDE TABLE

Italian, circa 1760–70
Carved and gilt wood;
marble top
105 × 153 × 74 cm
(41⁵⁄₁₆ × 60¼ × 29⅛ in.)
87.DA.135

The maker of this rare six-legged table was influenced
by the furniture designs of Giovanni Battista Piranesi, one of the principal forces behind the birth and
development of the Neoclassical style in Europe. As
in Piranesi's designs, this table combines antique ornaments with flamboyant, complex, and curvilinear elements. Against a wall in an eighteenth-century palazzo,
this table would have served to display decorative
objects or sculpture.

CLODION

(Claude Michel)
French, 1738–1814
*Vestal Presenting a Young
Woman at the Altar of Pan,*
circa 1775
Terracotta
H: 45.1 cm (17¾ in.)
85.SC.166

Through his technical brilliance and virtuoso handling
of wet clay, Clodion raised to new heights the aesthetic
quality of the terracotta as an independent work
of art rather than a preparatory sketch or model for a
sculpture in a more permanent material. The Museum's
terracotta depicts the enactment of a ritual before
a herm of Pan, the god of the fields, who is associated
with lust. The object's playful, romantic attitude toward
the classical world is typical of the work of Clodion,
who preferred genre scenes involving marginal mythological figures to the epic dramas of the principal
Olympian gods.

WORKSHOP OF
GEMINIANO COZZI

Italian, active 1764–1812
One of a Pair of Vases, 1769
Hybrid soft-paste porcelain
H: 29.8 cm (11¾ in.); DIAM
(max.): 27.3 cm (10¾ in.)
88.DE.9.1–.2

Produced in one of the leading Italian porcelain factories
of the eighteenth century, these vases are remarkable
for their large size, unusual shape, elaborate markings,
and delicately painted, sophisticated pictorial scheme.
The painted decoration on the pair, which copies contemporary print sources, celebrates the beauty and
sovereignty of the Venetian republic. One vase displays
the sea god Neptune on one side and an invented
riverside town on the other; the second vase shows the
allegorical figure of Venice and, on the other side, a
panorama of the Piazzetta San Marco.

FRANCESCO
ANTONIO
FRANZONI

Italian, 1734–1818
Table with Supports in
the Form of Winged Rams,
circa 1780
Marble
100 × 200 × 81 cm
(39½ × 79 × 32 in.)
93.DA.18

The artist of this table is best known for his work in the
Museo Pio-Clementino, Rome, the Vatican museum of
antiquities, in which Franzoni, under Pius VI, restored
ancient sculptures and decorative objects as well as
created works of his own design. It is in the *Sala degli
Animali* of this museum that Franzoni produced a pair
of tables nearly identical to the Getty Museum's example. These tables, whose supports include winged
rams and swags of laurel leaves, were undoubtedly
influenced by the works of Giovanni Battista Piranesi
(1720–1778). Franzoni was employed in Piranesi's
workshop upon his arrival in Rome around 1765 from
his native Carrara. The pier supports of the Museum's
example hold up a single slab of *Breccia Medicea*, a
massive and spectacular stone specimen from the Apu-
ane Alps, a quarry operated by the Medici from the
early seventeenth century.

JOSEPH NOLLEKENS

English, 1737 – 1823
Venus, 1773
Marble
H: 124 cm (48¹¹⁄₁₆ in.)
87.SA.106

Nollekens studied in Rome from 1762 to 1770, and his
style, a mannered classicism inflected by coy charm,
exhibits the influence of ancient and sixteenth-century
Italian sculpture. *Venus* is one of a group of female
deities by Nollekens in the Museum's collection. With
the other figures of Juno and Minerva, the *Venus*
formed part of a series sculpted for Lord Rockingham
to accompany a marble *Paris*, which Rockingham already owned and believed to be antique. The four statues together illustrate the story of the shepherd king
who was empowered to judge which goddess was the
fairest. Nollekens chose to depict each of the goddesses
in a different state of undress. Venus, the winner, is
nude except for the single sandal she is removing.

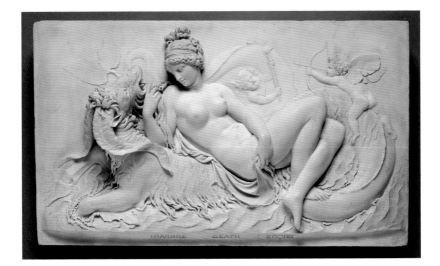

JOHN DEARE

English, active in London
and Rome, 1759–1798
*Venus Reclining on a
Sea Monster with
Cupid and a Putto*, 1785–87
Marble
33.7 × 54.8 cm (13¼ × 21⅝ in.)
98.SA.4

Deare was one of the most innovative British sculptors working in the Neoclassical style. In addition to incorporating motifs from ancient art, Deare was highly influenced by Italian sixteenth-century sculpture, which lent his style a languid sensuousness. This relief, showing Venus reclining on a fishtailed goat, recalls traditional Renaissance emblems of Lust. The Cupid and torch-bearing putto symbolize ardent desire. Venus entwines her fingers in the sea-goat's beard and the beast suggestively licks her hand, heightening the erotic tension inherent in the imagery. The monster's shaggy fur and the frothy waves of water are carved with the energy and precision typical of Deare's virtuoso technique.

ANTONIO CANOVA

Italian, 1757–1822
Apollo Crowning Himself,
1781–82
Marble
84.8 × 41.9 × 26.4
(33⅜ × 16½ × 10⅜ in.)
95.SA.71

Antonio Canova was the greatest Neoclassical sculptor from the 1790s until his death in 1822 and the most famous artist of his time. This marble of the nude god Apollo crowning himself with a laurel wreath was a pivotal work in the young sculptor's transition from a more naturalistic, Venetian style toward a Neoclassical aesthetic. *Apollo*'s pose conforms to a canonical *contrapposto*, in which the tensed limbs are opposite the relaxed limbs and the body reposes in harmonious equilibrium. Canova intended the figure to be a study in classical proportion that would emulate and rival antique statues. His subject, derived from Ovid's *Metamorphoses*, is a poignant and seldom-represented moment in the story of Apollo and Daphne showing Apollo's grief after the nymph has been transformed into a laurel tree.

JEAN-BAPTISTE
CARPEAUX

French, 1827–1875
Bust of Jean-Léon Gérôme,
1872–73
Marble
H (with socle): 61 cm (24 in.)
88.SA.8

Portrait sculptor to Napoleon III (reigned 1852–1871)
and a key figure in the history of nineteenth-century
sculpture, Carpeaux first modeled a bust of his friend
Gérôme, a prominent painter, in 1871, when the two
were exiles in London during the Paris Commune.
The Museum's bust is the only known marble example
of this portrait. In it Carpeaux achieved a romantic
image of the alienated, creative spirit in turmoil by
accentuating the sunken eyes and cheeks and giving full
play to the unruly mass of hair. The bust ends below
the neck with a jagged line that suggests a fragment or
a disembodied head.

VINCENZO GEMITO

Italian, 1852–1929
Medusa, 1911
Parcel-gilt silver
DIAM: 23.5 cm (9¼ in.)
86.SE.528

Vincenzo Gemito's gilt-silver *Medusa* is a sculpture in a category of its own, falling somewhere between a flat, two-sided medal and a fully sculpted object meant to be viewed from several angles. On the concave side the head of the Gorgon Medusa, one of three terrible, mythological sisters whose appearance was so hideous that their beholders were turned to stone, is modeled in relief, and the skin of a snake is rendered over the entire convex side. Gemito based his *Medusa* on an ancient cameo called the *Tazza Farnese*, which he could have studied in the Museo Archeologico Nazionale of his native city of Naples. The famous Hellenistic hard-stone object, a shallow bowl carved of agate, is decorated with the head of Medusa on its bottom. Although known primarily for his depictions of genre subjects— such as fisher boys, water-carriers, and gypsies— Gemito approached the theme of the Medusa head several times in his career, perhaps because its legendary power as a talisman attracted him, or because its long, abundant hair afforded him the opportunity to exploit his facility for sensuous, undulating lines.

Photographs

In mid-1984 the Museum established a new curatorial department dedicated to the art of photography. The opportunity to acquire several of the most important private collections of photographs in the world may be compared to the establishment of the Department of Manuscripts through the acquisition of the finest gathering of illuminated manuscripts then in private hands. The Museum decided to form a photography collection for reasons similar to those advanced in favor of collecting manuscripts and drawings: photography is an art fundamental to its time in which individual works of great rarity, beauty, and historical importance have been made.

Among the collections acquired in their entireties were those of Samuel Wagstaff, Arnold Crane, Bruno Bischofberger, and Volker Kahmen / George Heusch. The gathering of these collections, along with other block acquisitions made at the same time, including a substantial proportion of the collection of André Jammes, and a continuing program of individual acquisitions, has brought to Los Angeles the most comprehensive corpus of photographs on the West Coast.

The photographs reproduced in the *Handbook* represent a survey of some of the strengths of the collection, which is particularly rich in examples dating from the early 1840s and which includes major holdings by William Henry Fox Talbot, David Octavius Hill and Robert Adamson, Hippolyte Bayard, and other early practitioners in England who worked around Talbot, and in France. The collection also includes significant works by some of the most important photographers of the first half of the twentieth century. International in scope, its guiding principle is the belief in the supremacy of certain individual master photographers and in the timeless importance of individual master photographs.

For conservation reasons, photographs, like manuscripts and drawings, cannot be kept on permanent display. The collection is available to the public by appointment, and rotating exhibitions from the collection are shown in the photographs galleries at the Museum.

CHARLES R. MEADE

American, 1827–1858
*Portrait of Louis-Jacques-
Mandé Daguerre*, 1848
Half-plate daguerreotype
16 × 12 cm (6⅜ × 4¹¹⁄₁₆ in.)
84.XT.953.1

One of the unresolved mysteries in the history of photography is why Daguerre, who was a painter, became interested in light-sensitive materials about 1824. By 1829 he had formed a partnership with Nicéphore Niépce, who had successfully worked with sensitized metal plates. By New Year's Day, 1840, just four months after the first daguerreotype was exhibited in Paris, Daguerre's instruction manual had been translated into at least four languages and printed in at least twenty-one editions.

The daguerreotype was enthusiastically accepted in the United States. Charles R. Meade was the proprietor of a prominent New York photographic portrait studio. He made a pilgrimage to France in 1848 to meet the founder of his profession, and while there, he became one of the few people to photograph Daguerre.

UNKNOWN
AMERICAN
PHOTOGRAPHER

Edgar Allan Poe, late
May–early June 1849
Quarter-plate daguerreotype
12.2 × 8.9 cm (4 ¹³⁄₁₆ × 3 ½ in.)
84.XT.957

For reasons that are unclear, few daguerreotypes
of notable poets, novelists, or painters have survived
from the 1840s, and some of the best we have are
by unknown makers, as is the case with the Getty *Poe*.

Four of the eight times that Poe is known to have
been photographed occurred within the last year of
his life. This portrait was presented by him to Annie
Richmond, one of two women to whom he made romantic declarations in the months following the death
of his wife. Poe, who has been described as a libertine,
a drug addict, and an alcoholic, is represented here
as a man whose haunted eyes and disheveled hair reveal
the potential for mercurial emotions.

WILLIAM HENRY
FOX TALBOT

English, 1800 – 1877
Oak Tree in Winter, 1841
Salt print from paper negative
22.4 × 18.8 cm (8⅞ × 7⁷⁄₁₆ in.)
84.XM.893.1

Talbot's most important invention was one that is easily taken for granted today: the negative from which faithful replicas can be produced. He patented his procedure, which came to be known as the calotype process. He intended his invention to be clearly distinguished from the daguerreotype. Daguerre's procedure resulted in pictures on metal plates that could not be multiplied easily. Daguerreotypes were used almost exclusively for studio portraiture as sitters generally required but a single example, while calotypes required less fussy procedures and therefore were favored when a particular subject had an audience of more than one. There is no known early daguerreotype of a single tree. Yet trees were a favorite subject for photographers who were influenced by the aesthetic of picturesque romanticism evident in Talbot's treatment of this image.

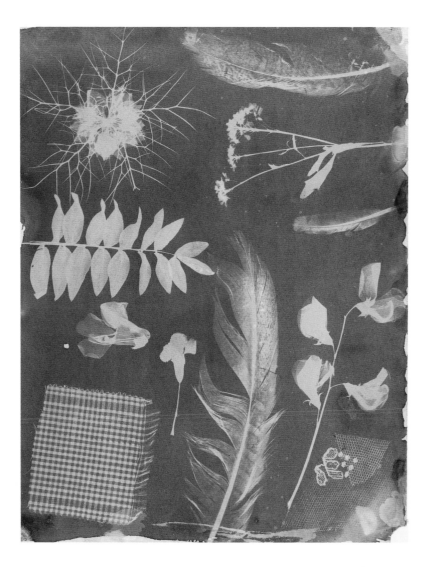

HIPPOLYTE BAYARD

French, 1801 – 1887
Arrangement of Specimens
(from Bayard Album),
circa 1841
Cyanotype
27.7 × 21.6 cm (10¹⁵⁄₁₆ × 8½ in.)
84.XO.968.5

Bayard occupies a position in the shadow of his fellow countryman Daguerre, and also of Talbot, from whom he learned some important techniques. Neither an inventor nor a follower, he was a satellite in the sphere of invention. Bayard was introduced to the work of Sir John Herschel and Talbot and soon abandoned his own direct-positive-on-paper prints in favor of Herschel's cyanotype and Talbot's calotype processes. Talbot was fascinated with nature's power to give form, while Bayard's arrangement of specimens seems to say that nature's design is elevated to a higher power by an organizing human intelligence. Both men proved that the choice of subject is fundamental to the art of photography.

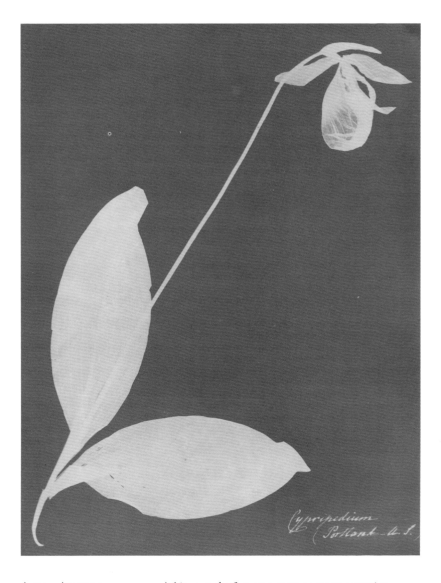

ANNA ATKINS

English, 1799 – 1871
Pink Lady's Slipper,
Collected in Portland
(Cipripedium), 1854
Cyanotype
25.8 × 20.2 cm
(10⅛ × 7¹⁵⁄₁₆ in.)
84.XP.463.3

Atkins was the first woman to create an extensive body of work. She came to the new medium through her father, John George Children, who presided over a February 1840 meeting of the Royal Society at which Talbot disclosed the workings of the positive-negative process. Children's friend Sir John Herschel instructed Atkins in the production of cyanotypes. Atkins combined Herschel's and Talbot's methods to create a visual lexicon of British ferns, algae, and plants, arranging her specimens in contact with light-sensitive paper and exposing the sheets to achieve cameraless negatives. From these negatives editions of positive cyanotype prints were made.

DAVID OCTAVIUS
HILL AND ROBERT
ADAMSON

Scottish, 1802 – 1870;
1821 – 1848
Newhaven Fisherman, 1845
Calotype
20.7 × 15 cm (8⅛ × 5¹⁵⁄₁₆ in.)
84.XM.445.1

Hill brought his abilities as a portrait painter to the
partnership in photography he formed with Adamson
in 1844. Adamson brought his skills in the manipula-
tion of the calotype process, which he had learned indi-
rectly from its inventor, William Henry Fox Talbot. In
the four years before Adamson's death the partners produced the first corpus of photographs made as art rather
than experiment. Their prints are characterized by a
Rembrandtesque chiaroscuro in tonalities enhanced by
gold chloride, which also gave the prints permanence.

SAMUEL BEMIS

American, 1789–1881
View of a Barn, 1840–41
Whole-plate daguerreotype
15.8 × 21.3 cm (6⅕₁₆ × 8⅜ in.)
84.XT.180.2

Samuel Bemis, a prosperous Boston dentist, summered in the early 1840s in the White Mountains region of New Hampshire, where he made some of the earliest American photographs of outdoor scenes. Bemis concentrated his attention on a small wooden barn, seemingly newly built, situated in an unidentified valley surrounded by a range of small mountains. The barn's construction is somewhat unusual in that its surface consists of vertical running planks butted edge to edge, but the most commanding aspect of this picture is less the design of the structure than the remarkable way in which its cubic essence is defined by light and shade. Bemis's selection of a homely barn and its surroundings as a subject contrasts with the choices made by his European contemporaries when they took their daguerrean equipment outdoors; they were more likely to focus on structures of great antiquity or historical importance.

JOHN PLUMBE, JR.

American (b. Wales),
1809 – 1857
The United States Capitol,
1846
Half-plate daguerreotype
10.8 × 13.9 cm
(4½ × 5½ in.)
96.XT.62

Plumbe's 1846 view of the east front of the United States Capitol is one of three he made of the building as part of a pioneering series documenting the principal buildings of Washington, which were then few in number. Although the building he shows is comparatively simple in contrast with the present day behemoth on the site, it had already had four architects: William Thornton, Benjamin Henry Latrobe, Charles Bulfinch, and Robert Mills. The dome is the work of Bulfinch, whose commission was the result of his earlier success with the Boston statehouse. The wings at the end of the building, which then housed the House of Representatives and the Senate, now serve as antechambers that connect the present chambers with the central rotunda and its dome. This is the only view Plumbe made of the building in which the White House is visible in the distance and is the only picture of any kind before 1900 that includes both monuments.

NADAR

(Gaspard-Félix Tournachon)
French, 1820 – 1910
Self-Portrait, circa 1854 – 55
Salt print
20.5 × 16.9 cm (8¹¹⁄₁₆ × 6⅝ in.)
84.XM.436.2

Before he dedicated himself to photography in the early 1850s, Nadar was — as he tells us in his autobiography — a poacher, a smuggler, a bureaucratic functionary, and a fighter for the cause of Polish liberation. *Nadar* was the nickname Gaspard-Félix Tournachon used in the 1840s to sign his stinging lithographic caricatures. While his drawings depended on bold exaggeration for their success, his photographs are marked by a spontaneous naturalism. Here, gentle light falls from above, leaving the right side of his face in partial darkness. His deeply shadowed eyes gaze at the observer, as though the camera did not exist. Equally expressive are his hands.

JULIA MARGARET CAMERON

English, 1815–1879
Ellen Terry at Age Sixteen,
negative, 1864; print,
circa 1875
carbon print
DIAM.: 24.1 cm (9½ in.)
86.XM.636.1

Cameron is renowned for her portraits of famous men such as Carlyle, Tennyson, and Herschel. This image of Ellen Terry, however, is one of her few known photographs of a female celebrity. Terry, the popular child actress of the British stage who later became Dame Ellen Terry, was sixteen years old when Cameron photographed her. She had just married the eccentric painter George Frederic Watts, who was thirty years her senior and an artistic mentor to Cameron. The ill-fated union lasted less than a year.

Cameron's portrait echoes Watts's study of Terry entitled *Choosing* (1864). Here, as in the painting, Terry is shown in profile with her eyes closed, an ultrafeminine, ethereal beauty in a melancholic dream state. In this guise she embodies the Pre-Raphaelite ideal of womanhood rather than the wild, boisterous teenager she was known to be. Terry's enchanting good looks, if not her personality, suited this ideal perfectly. The round format of the photograph, referred to as a tondo in painting, was popular among Pre-Raphaelite artists.

ALEXANDER
GARDNER

American, 1821–1882
*Lincoln on the Battlefield of
Antietam, Maryland*, 1862
Albumen print
22 × 19.6 cm (8⅝ × 7¾ in.)
84.XM.482.1

After the Second Battle of Bull Run, Robert E. Lee crossed the Potomac River in early September 1862 to occupy positions in Maryland and Virginia. The invasion was checked at Antietam by the forces of General George McClellan, whose failure to pursue Lee back across the river after the battle cost him his job.

Lincoln was the first American president to make time in his schedule to be photographed. Here we see him conferring with Major General John McClernand and Major Allan Pinkerton, who organized an espionage system behind Confederate lines. The genius of this photograph lies in Gardner's skillful composition built around the visual details of camp life. The tent and tent lines dominate. The eye is thus drawn equally to the fastenings on the lines and the faces of the principals. Despite compositional interruptions, the imposing figure of Lincoln remains the center of interest.

GUSTAVE LE GRAY

French, 1820–1882
*Cavalry Maneuvers,
Camp at Châlons*, 1857
Albumen print
31 × 36.7 cm (12⁷⁄₁₆ × 14⁷⁄₁₆ in.)
84.XO.377.12

Le Gray was a seasoned landscape and portrait photographer. In 1857 Napoleon III commissioned Le Gray to commemorate the inauguration of, and chronicle life in, the vast military camp established that year on the plain at Châlons-sur-Marne. Designed to accommodate twenty-five thousand imperial guards and staff, the camp sprawled over thirty thousand acres of mostly flat terrain. Le Gray's photographs are comprised of images of cavalry exercises on a grand scale and include genre studies of troops in bivouac, formal portraits of officers, records of ceremonies (including High Mass), and multipart overall panoramas of the camp as seen from the emperor's central pavilion. In this photograph, lines of cavalry behind a field bulwark are cloaked in an atmospheric mist new to photography. They occupy a narrow band across the center of the picture, leaving a great empty swath of pale sky and a dark, nearly vacant foreground. This photograph romanticizes the scene by miniaturizing the figures—a practical necessity to mitigate the blurring effect caused by men and horses in action.

HENRI–VICTOR REGNAULT

French, 1810–1878
Sèvres, the Seine at Meudon,
circa 1853
Carbon print by Louis-
Alphonse Poitevin
(French, 1819–1882)
31.1 × 42.5 cm
(12¼ × 16¹³/₁₆ in.)
92.XM.52

Regnault, a professor of physics at the Collège de France, where he performed classic experiments in thermodynamics and the properties of gases, obtained samples of Talbot's calotype printing papers from Jean-Baptiste Biot. Biot was the chief advocate of Talbot's method in France, and Regnault's good luck may have resulted from the meeting between Talbot and Biot in Paris in 1843. By 1852, the year before this negative was made, Regnault had become director of the porcelain factory at Sèvres and was hopeful that photographs could be as permanent as painted porcelain. This print was made with highly durable carbon ink using Alphonse Poitevin's carbon ink process, which was related to lithography.

This is an important complement to Silvy's *River Scene—La Vallée de l'Huisne* (see p. 289), where a similar interest in idyllic landscape composition related to the Barbizon School and early Impressionist painting is evident. Regnault experimented with different print-making processes. Using a waxed-paper negative, he created a print of great clarity. This unusual collaboration between Regnault and Poitevin is a carbon print made by that process's inventor. It is a benchmark in the history of the photomechanical printing of photographs.

CAMILLE SILVY

French, 1834–1910
*River Scene — La Vallée de
l'Huisne*, negative, 1858;
print, 1860s
Albumen print
25.7 × 35.6 cm (10⅛ × 14 in.)
90.XM.63

Silvy, who lived and worked in France and England in the 1850s and 1860s, is best known to the twentieth century through his *River Scene*. Inspired by painters of the Barbizon School, Silvy's four versions of this subject each show a different treatment of sky and atmosphere, changes that were achieved by utilizing multiple negatives and different toning methods. Silvy appears to have created two master negatives, one for the clouds and the other for the landscape. Some prints, including this one, may have been copied from the originals using skillfully made paper negatives that introduced a grainy image structure. This print was perhaps made in the 1860s, when the Barbizon School was giving way to Impressionism.

ROGER FENTON

British, 1819–1869
Pasha and Bayadère, 1858
Albumen print
45 × 36.3 cm (17¹¹/₁₆ × 14¼ in.)
84.XP.219.32

Even though his career as a photographer lasted only ten years, Roger Fenton had a strong impact on the history of the medium. A founder of what became the Royal Photographic Society, Fenton is best known for his images of the Crimean War, which were among the earliest photographic war reportage. He also made photographs that represent fictional situations. He often drew inspiration from painting, which he studied before turning to photography. In creating this image Fenton looked to the Orientalist works of, among others, Eugène Delacroix. These European depictions of the Islamic world were romanticized inventions rather than accurate representations of Middle Eastern life. Fenton's imaginary harem scene was staged in his London studio with his friends as models. The dancer's graceful pose was achieved with the aid of wires.

OSCAR GUSTAVE
REJLANDER

English (b. Sweden),
1813–1875
*The Infant Photography
Giving the Painter
an Additional Brush,*
circa 1856
Albumen print
6 × 7.1 cm (2⅜ × 2¹¹⁄₁₆ in.)
84.XP.458.34

Oscar Gustave Rejlander's allegory of painting is one
of the most direct treatments by a photographer in the
1850s of the interaction between painting and photography. Rejlander's title for this image refers to the idea
that an artist could use photographs of posed models
as preparatory studies for paintings. The photograph is
also a clever self-portrait, with the artist's own silhou-
ette reflected in a parabolic mirror. Like Fenton, Rejlander had been trained as a painter, and both his allegory
and Fenton's tableau on the facing page reflect the
efforts of British photographers of the period to make
the new art of photography more closely resemble the
traditional art of painting by adopting similar kinds
of subject material and pictorial tactics that both media
would share for the rest of the century. For artists the
camera miraculously enabled them to shorten the time
between having a perception and recording it in enormous detail.

CARLETON WATKINS

American, 1829–1916
Cape Horn, Columbia River, Oregon, negative, 1867; print, circa 1875
Albumen print by Isaiah West Taber
40.5 × 52.3 cm
(16⅛ × 20¹¹⁄₁₆ in.)
85.XM.11.2

While Watkins's Eastern contemporaries—Gardner and O'Sullivan—photographed the Civil War, Watkins, who ranks among the greatest American photographers, had the leisure in the tranquil West to ripen his style to full maturity between 1861 and 1868. Watkins had the gift to create complex compositions from very simple motifs and the power of perception to apprehend ephemeral forces in nature that form a seamless web of formal relationships. The three key elements of this picture are the massive rock formations, the transient quality of the boat loaded with a box of enormous fruit, and the delicacy of the light reflected from the water's surface.

Watkins designed photographs brilliantly to achieve a painterly interplay between surface pattern and spatial dimensions. The network of intricately connected compositional elements is chiefly responsible for this picture's palpable sense of space and is typical of this concern. Watkins's photographs were used as references by painters such as Thomas Hill and Albert Bierstadt.

Watkins was an excellent technician in a variety of materials. He frequently made stereographs, a type of miniature photograph that functioned for him as a sketching medium. After visualizing his subject, he would proceed to make mammoth plate negatives that yielded his celebrated presentation prints.

TIMOTHY O'SULLIVAN

American, 1840–1882
Desert Sand Hills near Sink of Carson, Nevada, 1867
Albumen print
22.3 × 29.1 cm (8¾ × 11½ in.)
84.XM.484.42

While employed by Alexander Gardner beginning in 1862, Timothy O'Sullivan was present at most of the chief military engagements of the Civil War, from the Second Battle of Bull Run to Appomattox. When Gardner published his *Photographic Sketch Book of the War* in 1865, forty-four of the one hundred photographs were by O'Sullivan — many of them simultaneously social documents and landscape compositions.

O'Sullivan left Gardner in 1867 to join the newly formed Fortieth Parallel Survey, the first federal exploring party in the West after the Civil War. O'Sullivan was allowed to roam the wilderness apart from the main party in order to prospect for motifs that would fulfill the Survey's scientific needs. We see here a kind of self-portrait showing the wagon that served as his rolling darkroom, pulled by four mules positioned on a hill of windblown sand near the Carson Sink, a shallow marshy region in western Nevada. The wagon has just made a U-turn, and the viewer sees the footprints leading from the vehicle to the spot where O'Sullivan erected his camera to compose this heroic image of exploration and discovery.

P. H. EMERSON

English, 1856–1936
Gathering Water Lilies, 1886
Platinum print
19.8 × 29.4 cm (7¹³/₁₆ × 11⁹/₁₆ in.)
84.XO.1268.10

"Wherever the artist has been true to nature, art has been good. Whenever the artist has neglected nature and followed his imagination, there has resulted bad art," P. H. Emerson wrote. Emerson called his aesthetic position Naturalism, and his preferred mode of presentation was the album or book, in which texts could accompany the photographs. One of his most important albums, *Life and Landscape of the Norfolk Broads*, was issued as a limited edition of carefully printed platinum photographs, mounted by hand onto pages, where *Gathering Water Lilies* was first seen. Emerson achieved compositional unity out of a great variety of competing elements that range from distracting reflections of light off the water, to the foreground branches, to the randomness of the lily pads and the river grasses. The composition is highly intuitive and yet admits to analysis. The structure of the photograph is built upon the diagonal axes that move corner to corner, from the bow through the stern of the wherry, and toward the opposite corners through the oars intersecting at the man's left hand, which is the center of the image. The point of sharpest focus is the surface of the woman's hat; its concentric circles of braided straw echo the circular field of focus established by the physics of lenses. "The image which we receive by the eye is like a picture minutely and elaborately finished in the center, but only roughly sketched in at the borders," Emerson wrote. This composition binds tender emotion to aesthetic form with poetic simplicity.

THOMAS EAKINS

American, 1844 – 1916
*Eakins's Students at the Site
for "The Swimming Hole,"*
circa 1883
Albumen print
16.5 × 12.2 cm (6½ × 4¾ in.)
84.XM.811.1

Photography was invented just when painters seemed
to require a new way of seeing the world. Although
many nineteenth-century painters dabbled in photography, very few carried their experiments far enough
to produce a significant corpus of work. Two painters
who did, and who are still universally respected, were
Thomas Eakins and Edgar Degas (see p. 296).

Eakins began to photograph in the late 1870s. Interested in the poses and gestures of static nude figures,
he made this study of seven young men at a swimming
hole around 1883. Male nudes were then very uncom-
mon in photography, and Eakins was among the first
to experiment with this subject. His models were
students at the Pennsylvania Academy of the Fine Arts,
which censored him for this practice. Eakins's painting *The Swimming Hole*, now in the Amon Carter
Museum, Fort Worth, was created from sketches based
on these photographs; it is probably the most famous
nineteenth-century painting known to have been based
on a photograph.

EDGAR DEGAS

French, 1834–1917
*After the Bath, Woman
Drying Her Back*, 1896
Gelatin silver print
16.5 × 12 cm (6¹¹/₁₆ × 4¾ in.)
84.XM.495.2

Degas was an inveterate experimenter in the graphic arts, creating major works in monotype, drawing, etching, and lithography before turning his talents to photography between 1894 and 1896. However, twenty-five years before, at about the time he first met Nadar, Degas used carte-de-visite photographs as the sources for several portraits. In 1874 he drew a pastel of a dancer posing in a photographer's studio, which led to his 1896 study of a model drying herself after her bath. The movement shown here is complex and contorted, almost acrobatic. The photograph is related to a startling, almost voyeuristic series of drawings devoted to the motions of women dressing, bathing, and twisting their bodies while drying themselves.

FREDERICK H. EVANS

English, 1853–1943
*Kelmscott Manor: In the Attics
(No. 1)*, 1896
Platinum print
15.5 × 20.2 cm (6⅛ × 7¹⁵⁄₁₆ in.)
84.XM.444.89

Evans found poetic and artistic inspiration in the architecture of the past. He was inspired by the nearness of the designer-craftsmen of the Middle Ages to their product and by the essential equality of the craftsmen to each other. In 1896 Evans visited the home of William Morris, the proselytizing medievalist. Kelmscott Manor dates from 1280 and is highly representative of the medieval manor house, an institution in which the role of the craftsman was central to all of everyday life. Evans methodically photographed the exterior and interior and selected decorations, including the attics.

Evans photographed architecture and its ornaments using a vocabulary of light, volume, and texture. In this photograph he isolates the intersecting network of posts and beams, choosing his point of view carefully so as to make clear that they were carved by hand out of the trunks and branches of trees. Almost a decade later, Evans wrote that he hoped people would exclaim upon seeing his photographs, "What a noble, beautiful, fascinating building that must be, and how priceless an art is that sort of photography that can so record one's emotional rapprochement to it!" In focusing his attention on the details of architecture, Evans proved that a photographer could join in a single artistic temperament the classic and the romantic, the linear and the painterly, the objective and the abstract.

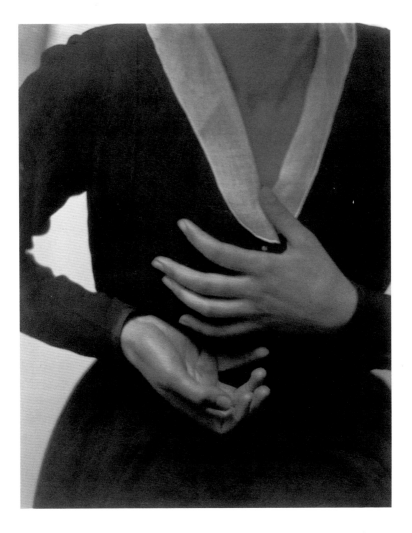

ALFRED STIEGLITZ

American, 1864–1946
Georgia O'Keeffe: A Portrait,
June 4, 1917
Platinum print
24.4 × 19.5 cm (9⅝ × 7¹¹⁄₁₆ in.)
91.XM.63.3

A catalyst for Stieglitz was Georgia O'Keeffe, a young painter whose art and personal style influenced him and his circle enormously. She was living in New York during the first half of 1916 and was included in a group exhibition at Stieglitz's gallery. Toward the end of the exhibition she visited the gallery for the first time, appearing "thin, in a simple black dress with a little white collar [and with] a sort of Mona Lisa smile," as Stieglitz recalled. This study was among the first of a series that eventually amounted to more than 325 photographs of O'Keeffe that probed different aspects of her persona. Hands are an important motif in the series. Stieglitz shows us hands that shape art, and he challenges us to imagine how they could also stroke and caress, grasp and hold, or scratch and claw. In visual language they stand for everything in nature that is subject to change.

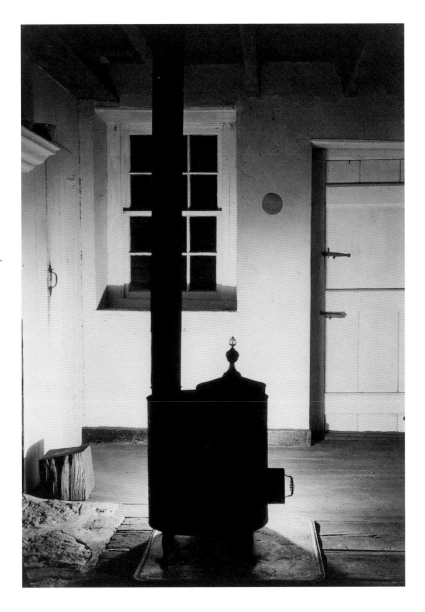

CHARLES SHEELER

American, 1883–1965
Doylestown House—
The Stove, 1917
Gelatin silver print
22.9 × 16.2 cm (9 × 6⅜ in.)
88.XM.22.1

This photograph displays a concern for the symbolic value of pure light, along with the status of the found object in the spirit of Duchamp. The interior is photographed at night, with a single source of artificial light blasting from the belly of the stove via the electric bulbs that had recently come into use by photographers. Sheeler reconciles the perennially opposing forces of light and dark, of mass and line, and of nostalgia and modernity. "[The photographs are] probably more akin to drawings than to my photographs of paintings and sculptures," wrote Sheeler to Stieglitz.

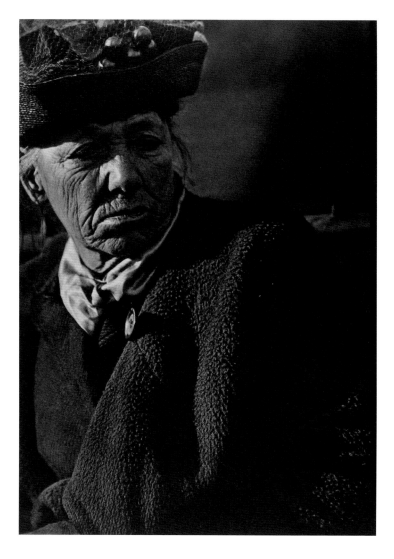

PAUL STRAND

American, 1890–1976
Portrait—New York, 1916
Platinum print
34.3 × 25.1 cm (13½ × 9⅞ in.)
89.XM.1.1

When Strand first visited Stieglitz in 1910, he had been listening to the advice of Lewis Hine, who was one of the most socially concerned photographers of the twentieth century. One of Strand's contributions to a new aesthetic was to bring together Hine's humanism with Stieglitz's formalism (see p. 298). This photograph made in New York's Washington Square Park is less a portrait than an archetype of old age and urban survival. The woman has been photographed without her knowledge. The composition is off-center, with hard-edged light and an oblique viewpoint that establishes a sense of sculptural immobility. Strand turned to socially conscious themes in the 1930s and never returned to complete abstraction.

DOROTHEA LANGE

American, 1895–1965
*Migrant Mother,
Nipomo, California,* 1936
Gelatin silver print
34.3 × 26.7 cm
(13⅞ × 10⅜ in.)
98.XM.162

One of the most respected photographers of the New Deal era, Dorothea Lange's photographs eloquently captured the desperation of poverty-stricken Americans during the Great Depression.

At a pea-pickers' camp in Cayuma valley in San Luis Obispo County, Lange photographed a woman of Cherokee descent from Oklahoma who was living with her husband and seven children, eking out a livelihood from the land. On the back of this print Lange inscribed the following: "This family had just sold the tent from over their heads and the tires from their car to buy food. . . . They were living in an open field, [in] cold and rainy weather, in the hope of getting some work to do picking peas, along with hundreds of other families."

Lange's photographs were designed to effect social change and, in a modest way, they did. She subtitled this picture *Facing Starvation* and considered it part of a larger project on the subject of migrant labor that she called "Human Erosion in California."

ANDRÉ KERTÉSZ

American (b. Hungary),
1894–1985
Chez Mondrian, 1926
Gelatin silver print
10.9 × 7.9 cm (4⁵⁄₁₆ × 3⅛ in.)
86.XM.706.10

The Hungarian-born Kertész once described himself as a "Naturalist-Surrealist." In his most characteristic photographs, an abiding interest in the prosaic aspects of life blends with a surrealistic perspective. His work is marked by an ability to surprise us by addressing familiar subjects in unusual ways. If the subject was a still life, Kertész chose his viewpoint deftly and occasionally made a subtle alteration to gain his desired effect. He described for a friend the shaping of this particular composition: "The door to [Mondrian's] staircase was always shut, but as I opened it in my mind's eye the two sights started to present themselves as two halves of an interesting image that I thought should be unified. I left the door open, but to get what I wanted I had to move a sofa."

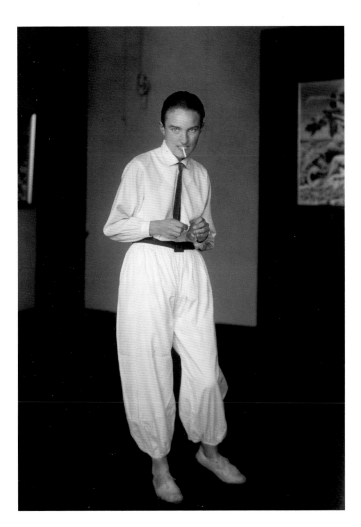

AUGUST SANDER

German, 1876–1964
*Frau Peter Abelen,
Cologne,* 1926
Gelatin silver print
23 × 16.3 cm (9¹⁄₁₆ × 6⁷⁄₁₆ in.)
84.XM.498.9

Enigmatically, Sander's photographs are simultaneously traditional and modern. He used a tripod-mounted plate camera when handheld cameras were attracting many photographers, and he usually posed his figures in an environment that revealed something about their life, a strategy appropriated from painting and professional portraiture. Sander was skilled at causing his subjects to project a sense of expectation and then arresting that moment. Dressed in stylish culottes, Frau Peter Abelen stands in a gallery surrounded by her husband's paintings. She is about to light the cigarette between her teeth with the match and striker she holds. We have a powerful sense of tense psychological reality. The woman is androgynous, and her expression falls somewhere between anticipation and anger. We do not know whether Sander accuses or praises her.

EDWARD WESTON

American (1886–1958)
Two Shells, May 1927
Gelatin silver print
24 × 18.4 cm (9½ × 7¼ in.)
88.XM.56

Tabletop still-life arrangements were a favorite subject for amateur photographers, but very few achieved the powerful form and masterful control of technique that Weston did. Bored with portraiture, he experimented with the symbolic and formal potential of found objects. By nesting one chambered nautilus shell inside another, he created a powerful form not seen in nature. Viewing his subject close-up from below, with a camera designed for eight-by-ten-inch sheets of film, Weston was challenged to keep all the visual elements in sharp focus. He wrote: "It is this very combination of the physical and spiritual in a shell . . . which makes it such an important abstract of life."

ALBERT RENGER-
PATZSCH

German, 1897–1966
*Flatirons for Shoe
Manufacture*, circa 1928
Gelatin silver print
23 × 17 cm (9¹/₁₆ × 6¹¹/₁₆ in.)
84.XM.138.1

In choosing such unexpected subjects as industrial artifacts, Renger-Patzsch risked having their meaning
misunderstood, for he was expressing himself as a poet,
not as a reporter. Like the lyrical poet, the photographer possesses an acute and exhilarating respect for the
eminence and reality of the object; the new object
that has been created in the form of a photograph has
no other reason to exist than the pleasure it brings.
Poet-photographers make up their own language from
picture to picture and keep us interested in spare
and unusual compositions by not photographing in the
ways we expect. The poetic photograph has the power —
sometimes brutally direct — to create deep and
unnameable feelings about commonplace objects.

EUGÈNE ATGET

French, 1857–1927
Staircase, Montmartre, 1924
Albumen print
21.8 × 17.8 cm (8⁹⁄₁₆ × 7 in.)
90.XM.124.1

Atget created this study of a group of apartments in 1924, the same year Berenice Abbott first saw one of his photographs and became the most devoted apostle of his art. Trees were a favorite Atget subject, and this elegant and well-proportioned specimen stands in definite contrast to another favorite subject, architecture. In this block we see neither noble materials nor heroic design but rather journeyman production that attempts to reconcile utility and beauty. The eye is teased by the elegance of the leafless tree that dominates the picture; it is intrigued by the askew chimney pipes and by an agglomeration of textures ranging from mildew to decaying wood and from decomposing plaster to scarred stone. The tree by comparison seems ageless, like the sculpture at its base.

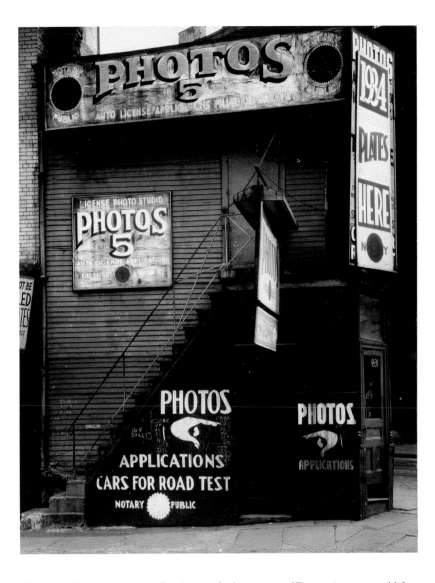

WALKER EVANS

American, 1903–1975
License Photo Studio,
New York, 1934
Gelatin silver print
18.2 × 14.4 cm (7 3/16 × 5 11/16 in.)
84.XM.956.456

Best known for his images of Depression-era rural life,
Walker Evans was a pivotal figure in American docu-
mentary-style photography. His seminal work of 1938,
American Photographs, includes eighty-seven images of
people, architecture, and vernacular art made over
a decade in the eastern United States and Cuba. Osten-
sibly a proclamation of American culture, the book's
underlying theme is photography itself. Evans presented
the photographs in a sequence intended to be "read."
This view of a run-down photo studio is the opening
image. With it Evans set the tone for the entire book.
The harsh frontal view, unidealized subject, and
fascination with commercial signs recur throughout.

MANUEL ALVAREZ
BRAVO

Mexican, b. 1902
*The Good Reputation
Sleeping 1, 2, 3*, 1938–39
Gelatin silver prints
Each: 8.8 × 18.9 cm
(3½ × 7⁷⁄₁₆ in.)
92.XM.23.37

Alvarez Bravo created this version of the work he called
La buena fama durmiendo—the only one to survive
in its original three-part format—at the suggestion of
André Breton. Breton was in Mexico City in 1939 to
help organize an exhibition of Surrealist art at the
Galería de Arte Mexicano. Alvarez Bravo imagined his
triptych as the cover of the exhibition catalogue. The
negatives were made on the roof of the national arts
school. As the photographer recalled on a visit to Los
Angeles in 1992, the bandages were supplied by a physi-
cian friend, and the symbolic cactus pears were pro-
cured from a local outdoor market by the school porter.
Posed in bright sunlight in a position of unnatural
vulnerability, the model has been dressed in a costume
that focuses our attention on the tufts of pubic hair,
which caused censors to declare the work unacceptable
for reproduction on the cover.

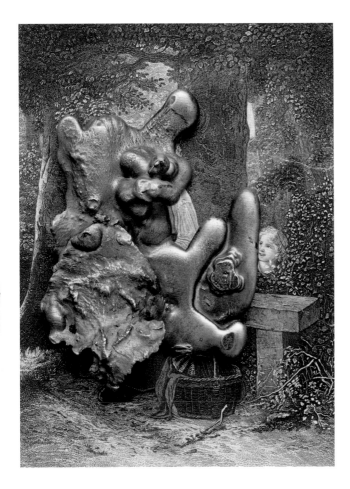

FREDERICK
SOMMER

American (b. Italy, 1905)
*Virgin and Child with Saint
Anne and the Infant Saint
John*, 1966
Gelatin silver print
24 × 17.7 cm (9⁷⁄₁₆ × 6¹⁵⁄₁₆ in.)
94.XM.37.39

Working in a singular style informed by the contradic-
tory sources of Dada and Surrealism and West Coast
naturalism, Sommer's approach to photography is
encapsulated in his statement: "If you can really understand why you take a photograph, you don't do it.
You do it for the margin of the unstated . . . you hope
to be able to come back to it—and find a wider statement." Sommer has made an art of collecting refuse
that he has carefully selected and then studied for years,
sometimes even decades, before finding a place for it
in his art. The peculiarly formed lump of metal that
appears in this photograph was once part of the melted
remains of a burned-out, wrecked automobile. By combining it with a Victorian book illustration, Sommer
invites us to recall Leonardo da Vinci's painting of the
same name. If the word imagination means "one thing
seen in the form of another," this is a perfect example of
the photographer's imaginative process.